BUT WAIT, THERE'S MORE

BUT WAIT, THERE'S MORE

DISCOVERING
everything you never knew
you always wanted in
JESUS

DONNA BOWDEN NASH

Trilogy Christian Publishers

A Wholly Owned Subsidiary of Trinity Broadcasting Network

2442 Michelle Drive

Tustin, CA 92780

Copyright © 2024 by Donna Bowden Nash

Unless otherwise noted, Scripture quotations are taken from the *Holy Bible, New American Standard Version,* Copyright 1995 by the Lockman Foundation. Used by permission. All rights reserved. Scripture quotations marked ESV are taken from the ESV Bible (*The Holy Bible*, English Standard Version). Copyright 2001 by Crossway, a publishing ministry of Good News Publishers. Used by permission. All rights reserved. Scripture quotations marked NIV are taken from *The Holy Bible, New International Version.* Copyright 2011 by Biblica, Inc. Used by permission of Zondervan. All rights reserved. Scripture quotations marked NKJV are taken from the *New King James Version.* Copyright 1982 by Thomas Nelson. Used by permission. All rights reserved. Scripture quotations marked NLT are taken from *The Holy Bible, New Living Translation.* Copyright 2015 by Tyndale House Foundation. Used by permission of Tyndale House Ministries, Carol Stream, Illinois 60188. All rights reserved. Scripture quotations marked MSG are taken from *The Message.* Copyright 2018 by Eugene H. Peterson. Used by permission of NavPress. All rights reserved. Represented by Tyndale House Publishers, a division of Tyndale House Ministries. Scripture quotations marked TPT are taken from *The Passion Translation.* Copyright 2017 by BroadStreet Publishing Group, LLC. Used by permission. All rights reserved.

All rights reserved, including the right to reproduce this book or portions thereof in any form whatsoever.

For information, address Trilogy Christian Publishing

Rights Department, 2442 Michelle Drive, Tustin, Ca 92780.

Trilogy Christian Publishing/ TBN and colophon are trademarks of Trinity Broadcasting Network.

For information about special discounts for bulk purchases, please contact Trilogy Christian Publishing.

Trilogy Disclaimer: The views and content expressed in this book are those of the author and may not necessarily reflect the views and doctrine of Trilogy Christian Publishing or the Trinity Broadcasting Network.

10 9 8 7 6 5 4 3 2 1

Library of Congress Cataloging-in-Publication Data is available.

ISBN 979-8-89333-441-8

ISBN 979-8-89333-442-5 (ebook)

For Dad
Richard H. Bowden
July 28, 1946–April 1, 2019

ACKNOWLEDGMENTS

Thank You, Jesus, for being King of my heart, Lord of my life, and my Substitute in death. Father God, thank You for curating an amazingly beautiful life for me and sacrificing Your Son for me. Thank You, Holy Spirit, for the power within me to write Your message of More.

Thank you, Brody, for your love and support and for giving me the green light for this project. Thank you, Paisley and Ziva, for your patience. Thank you, Kameron, for challenging me to be better than I am. Thank you, Mom, for being an amazing mom and grandma. Thank you, Bowden and Nash clans, for walking with me to today.

Thank you, prayer partners, for being there when I need to refocus and for calling out to Jesus on my behalf.

Thank you, Whitney, Judy, Alethea, and Zach, for Fridays at 10:30 MST. Thank you, Zach, for your kind words, challenging teaching, and helping me steer clear of false teaching.

Thank you to the staff of Trilogy Christian Publishing for your assistance, guidance, and expertise.

Table of Contents

Foreword 11

Introduction. 13

Chapter 1 17

Chapter 2 23

Chapter 3 31

Chapter 4 37

Chapter 5 41

Chapter 6 49

Chapter 7 55

Chapter 8 57

Chapter 9 63

Chapter 10 67

Chapter 11 77

Chapter 12 83

Chapter 13 91

Chapter 14 101

Chapter 15 109

Chapter 16 119

Chapter 17 127

Chapter 18 137

Chapter 19 145

Chapter 20 157

Chapter 21 165

Epilogue 171

Appendix 179

Endnotes 181

About the Author 185

Foreword

By Zach Sloane

The recurring themes in this book of gratitude to God for who He is and what He has done, coupled with what can only be understood as Donna's deep desire to know Jesus in His fullness and help others do the same, make this a must-read book.

In the book of Philippians, the apostle Paul wrote what has become the rallying cry for all who want to know God for who he really is and for all willing to push past what is familiar and comfortable. He said, "Not that I have already attained, or am already perfected; but I press on, that I may lay hold of that for which Christ Jesus has also laid hold of me" (Phillippians 3:12, NKJV).

What I love about Donna opening up her own process and discovery of the more that Jesus has for her is that as I read her journey, I feel myself wanting to, needing to, and being inspired to go along on a similar journey myself. Paul gave us this wonderful biblical language for pressing on into all God has, and in her book *But Wait, There's More*, Donna helps us discover not only what that might look like in the twenty-first century but outlines some of the common pitfalls and obstructions that can box us in and keep us from believing there is more, much less reaching out to Jesus and daring to believe we can experience it.

Personally, I come from a very expressive and faith-fueled Christian background, a faith tradition that often prides itself on believing in God to do more, to move amongst His people in ways that surprise, inspire, and stretch our faith. One thing I have found, though, to be too often true is that in this environment and its embrace of God's More, sometimes that pursuit can become a formulaic, one-size-fits-all prescription for not only our own personal relationships with Jesus but also for what the More He has for us must look like in our homes, families, and churches. If we are not careful, our quest for More can become an exercise in discrediting and dishonoring where we have come from, who we have journeyed with this far, and undervaluing what we know and have from God up to this point. This book navigates this tension beautifully, reaching out for more while leaning into what you already have, inviting others along the way, and honoring those God has put in our lives while calling us to stretch our horizons.

As one who is also in the faith-fueled pursuit of all that God has for us, I can so strongly recommend this book because although it is challenging, and it confronts our assumptions regarding our status quo, it skillfully does so with a heart full of honor and gentleness that has sacrificed neither passion nor abandon. In this book, there is incredible respect for our journeys, and it makes space for the individuality of God's call and connection with each of us through Jesus Christ. Donna beautifully honors the person and work of Holy Spirit and the Scriptures, acknowledges the sometimes hard road of forging faith in community, and, throughout the book, shares the inviting vulnerability of one who is walking the walk. This book has been written to Jesus to get in His people what He paid such a dear price to see us walk in: something exceedingly and abundantly more than we have yet to ask or even dare imagine. Something available to each one of us according to His Spirit's power at work within.

Introduction

There's More, I tell you, there is More. There is more than can be written. There is more to a relationship with Jesus than can be shared within the pages of any book, secular or spiritual. There is more than can be felt. There is a fullness of life that you may be missing. There is a way of being in which the manifestation of abundance is experienced daily. This feeling of abundance is accompanied by contentment and satisfaction in whatever that day may bring. Do you experience abundance daily? There is more to life than living and dying. There is more to life than raising children or succeeding in business. There is more to be unlocked within you than you can currently grasp. More does not have to equate to accumulating things. Please do not expect more things. Expect more beyond things. More can be found in your state of being. More is found in intimacy with Jesus Christ. More can be exchanged for the "less" that you are living in.

More can be unlocked by anyone anytime, but you must choose your more: more of the same old world that we wake up to every day is less than God wants you to experience. Would you like the immeasurably more that comes in Jesus Christ through the power of Holy Spirit? With Holy Spirit, you can know more goodness, more patience, more kindness, more celebration, more growth, more mercy, more blessing, more peace, more love, and more joy. With Holy Spirit comes more freedom, more reasons for living, more awe, more wonder, and more power through His indwelling in your life. He wants to give you more talents and blessings that you can share with your world. He wants to give you more words to counsel, share, minister, and comfort. He wants you to know that there is more to see, more that should be heard, more to be touched, more that you can feel, and more to taste.

"A thief has only one thing in mind—he wants to steal, slaughter, and destroy. But I have come to give you everything in abundance, more than you expect—life in its fullness until you overflow!" (John 10:10, TPT)

Right there in black and white, found in the pages of Scripture, is the dichotomy of more and less. Everyone has access to more, but most allow their more to be stolen.

Choosing more pain, disappointment, fear, anxiety, and heartache is your other option. No one will likely admit to choosing these things, but a choice is made that will lead to these, to less. When you choose self, family, friends, work, things, hobbies, or entertainment over the lordship of Jesus Christ, a clear choice is made. Placing Jesus Christ in second place gives our enemy, Satan, permission to steal, kill, and destroy any aspect of our lives. Much of that comes naturally, or at least effortlessly, as we walk through this sin-cursed Earth and experience natural consequences, but there is more of that to be found also. The lie we buy into, though, is that we can gain, accumulate, or experience More without Holy Spirit in our lives. We try, and at first, some of us find more, or temporary happiness, in material things and experiences. Following the world's formula for finding more—which requires putting money, a person or people, self, or accomplishment on a pedestal—leads to being robbed of peace, joy, time, and hope. Many times, even life itself is stolen from us, either in poor health or the death of a loved one.

One of the greatest lies that we accept and live in throughout our lives is that this world is as good as it gets and that the afterlife will be boring in heaven and a party in hell. This is one of the many mental entanglements that needs to be unknotted. This is one of the lies told to us by the secular culture all around us, causing us to be short-sighted and not live in light of eternity. We are desensitized by the influence of a world that demands instant gratification, results now, and reminds us that "there is a time to be born and a time to die" (Ecclesiastes 3:2, NIV). With a proper view of eternity, our choice between More and Less becomes much clearer, and choosing the More that God has for you is simply that: a choice. Heaven promises the fullness of relationship, creativity, provision, peace, and His perfect Presence. Hell is an excruciating separation from God.

"Choose…today whom you will serve" (Joshua 24:15, NASB). Choose today. This is not about a choice you made when you were five, fifteen, or last Sunday. This is about choosing Christ today, tomorrow, and the next. Choose to love Him. Choose to serve Him. Honor Him with your choices. This implies that He is above you, He is Who you are working for, He is calling the shots. Choose Him, and He will unlock the "immeasurably more" that is mentioned in Ephesians 3:20 (NIV). The more often you make this choice, the easier it becomes. Choosing God, Jesus, and Holy Spirit over yourself, family, friends, jobs, or your other idols is usually a difficult choice, but so worth it. This will unlock so much for you that you cannot fathom.

More is found in both the "here and now" and in eternity. Perhaps you believe the lie that life on Earth is where we "go for broke," "shoot for the stars," "go all in," or "seize the day" because we are not promised tomorrow. While we are indeed not promised tomorrow here on Earth, we are promised a tomorrow. For those who have placed their faith and trust in Jesus Christ, the tomorrow promised will be better than today. For those who have placed their faith and trust in Jesus Christ and have chosen to serve Him this day, More is promised. More is found in the balanced perspective of yesterday, today, and tomorrow. Sometimes More can be seen in the ease of your job, plans coming together effortlessly, having an experience that you have been waiting for, or simply the unexpected, perfectly-timed text of encouragement from a friend.

Balance. The American mindset is one of either/or, pros and cons, good and evil, best and worst. Consider the possibility that More is found in the balance of both/and. Charles Dickens outlined a reality where the best and worst of times were simultaneously realized. We can embrace this reality as well. More is found in balance. Although More may seem to have the potential to tip the scale of either/or, best/worst, good/evil, more actually can be found right in the middle. More can be found in the space between the period at the end of "It was the best of times" and "It was the worst of times." More realized within the parameters of both/and has much greater potential than that of either/or. The church in America has fostered a mindset of either/or, but Jesus calls us to both/and. Jesus calls us to a life of More, and the door to More is Holy Spirit.

In the pages to follow, we will discuss how many followers of Christ are living lives of Less. We speak and sing of God's wonders, abundance, faithfulness, and goodness, but our lives look just like everyone else's: ordinary, sprinkled with some highs, lows, and answered prayers. We, especially in American culture, have accepted lives of less, are comfortable in lives of less, and rarely seek the Lord for more. Scripture speaks of more, immeasurably more. Our loving Heavenly Father wants us to seek Him for More in life. He has designed More for you that is unique to you. Your blessings, favor, and opportunities will not look like anyone else's. As original as your fingerprint is, so is the story God has written for you to walk into—a life of immeasurably more. *But Wait, There's More* will allow you to discover everything you never knew you always wanted in a life walking with Jesus Christ. Journey into a deep relationship with the Father, Son, and Holy Spirit as you identify and deconstruct the framework of spiritual development you were raised in and reconstruct it into a life of abundance and more than you have ever asked Him for or imagined.

Chapter 1

You are made for More. You are wired for More. Wherever you are, whatever your name or title is, and however hard or easy your life is right now, you were created to experience More, Immeasurably More than all you could ask for or even imagine. I know this because Ephesians 3:20 tells me so. I know this because God has shown me this personally. I know how you can discover the Immeasurably More that God has in store for you. I want to help you discover your More. Your More will not look like mine. Your More should look different than the blessings bestowed on your neighbor, friend, co-worker, or family member. Our God is a meticulous, abundantly generous curator of life and will give you the More that is designed for the unique life He desires for you to have: a full, rewarding, and truly blessed life.

More in Christ is found through simple practices, not in a prescribed formula or recipe, mind you, but in choosing Him daily. You can find the path that God has carved out just for you. Create a unique recipe for More. Discovering the ingredients for your recipe of More is why this book is in your hands. Once you discover the components, keys, tools, and simple truths for discovering More, you will be equipped to write your recipe for more with your Maker, Savior, and Best Friend. As I discovered these truths and tools, I was reminded of Lois Lowry's *The Giver* because discovering More was like going beyond the black-and-white limits of my upbringing into a world full of color and life beyond the framework of my theology.

Discovering your More is essentially as simple as:

1. sitting in God's presence
2. walking with Christ

3. standing in the power Holy Spirit gives you.

Consider how God uses these simple verbs of sitting, walking, and standing in Psalm 1 to light a path that leads to a greater depth of intimacy. Discovering the gift of More through these simple practices is essentially easy but will take commitment, and challenges can be expected. Keeping your gums healthy is essentially easy, but you have to brush and floss. A couple of tools and a little bit of time is all that is needed, but consistency is key. Just like cleaning your teeth is more effective with a brush, toothpaste, floss, and a few minutes, so is getting to know the Father, Son, and Holy Spirit. If all you have is water, your finger, and ten seconds, that is still better than neglecting to scrub your teeth. Strides can be made with simple tools and truths. A scripture verse on a post-it note in your bathroom mirror can transform you spiritually over a couple of weeks as you study it while brushing your teeth—possibly more so than a forty-minute sermon you were ignoring on Sunday as you scrolled through a list of emails on your phone. Quality and consistency are key to discovering the gift of More that God has for you. Quality and consistency will do far more for you than quantity and random engagement with the Lord and Spirit at a Sunday morning sermon, Christian concert, or conference.

Challenges will come in "harnessing more" to meet our bandwidth and seeing if the ingredients for "our recipe" can be found in the cupboards of our education, culture, and family structure. How do we encapsulate More in our walks with Christ when there is so much comfort in the boundaries or scaffolding of how God first revealed Himself to us? There needs to be some intentional manipulation. Manipulation is often used so negatively, and surely, some have been manipulated by people within the church in horrible ways. Manipulation, though, is what takes place when we are molded. Manipulation can set straight what has shifted out of place.

We need to embrace a vocabulary that allows us to see beyond the framework we were given throughout our upbringing. We need to break free from our preconceived notions and ideas of religion and relationship with Jesus Christ. The framework of our spiritual beliefs and ideas was never intended by Holy Spirit to be walls that imprisoned us. God gives us a framework to guide us as we grow. This framework is a product of the family, culture, and education we have been given. Once mature, we can break free from that framework or scaffolding and grow in grace and Truth beyond our wildest imaginations.

Other challenges will come from the enemy. He will entangle us in distractions and half-truths and will steal time from us. God can equip us with the countermeasures we need to combat these attacks. God is able to give discernment, wisdom, strength, truth and can miraculously redeem time when we give the battle to Him. We must trust Him fully and not lean on our own understanding, which has been tainted by the world and our enemy.

Our God is a God of both the simple and the complex, of both the foolish and the profound. However, He is not in the habit of informing us where He finds us on that continuum. He will not turn you away from a blessing because you need His truth simplified. God will show you a translation, author, or teacher who will place the proverbial cookies on a lower shelf for you. Then, as Ephesians 1:17–19 tells us, He will give you wisdom, knowledge, enlightenment, hope, and understanding of the riches of His glory and the surpassing greatness of His power. Wow. I know this to be true. God has done this exact thing in the life of a loved one of mine. God can grant proverbial "whitening strips" for the soul to remove twenty-five years of coffee stains.

The world offers more, and Jesus Christ offers Immeasurably More. The more the world offers is temporary and fades with time. Jesus offers More with eternal benefits. Is this a win-win situation? Does this somehow relate to the phrase "less is more"? Sometimes less is a good thing, right? Less calories. Less stress. Less work. What would less look like in this construct? Does less need to be acknowledged in this discussion? Yes. Less is putting the book down now, choosing to remain the same, choosing to keep on keeping on because life is not all bad. There is a lot of good in this world if you look. Looking at life through the mindset of the world, through a framework that is entangled with weeds of sin, will cause you to live in Less. You are likely blind to those weeds because they have always been there, and you don't know what life is like without them. They plague us all, even the most righteous of Christians. They started growing in Eden. Less is continuing in the tradition, routine, and ritual of religion that brings peace, contentment, joy, and a heart full of love, but these come with conditions or an expiration date. How can peace, contentment, joy, and love be Less? The difference is in a blend of quality and quantity. The enemy wants you content where you are and not pursuing More. Less is realized when you don't pursue More and sit in what you have in front of you. Less is not the opposite of More but one step below or behind More. You are living in Less. I live in Less some days. More is found in the pursuit. More is found in today's pursuit of the Kingdom of God and His Righteousness. More is found in tomorrow. More is found in eternity.

"Seek first the Kingdom of God and His Righteousness and all these things will be added to you" (Matthew 6:33, ESV).

Come find More with me. Let's talk about discovering everything you never knew you always wanted in a relationship with Jesus. Continue on this journey with me. Through wonder, awe, investigation, and testing, we will set our minds on righteousness and eternity. Waiting, or at least a pause of recognition, comes before More. Pause, insert a "but" into your story that will allow you to slow down and recognize all that God has in store for you. Discover your "recipe for More," and then feast on the banquet of blessing that He has prepared for you.

Chapter 2

Framework. What's your framework? What makes you unique? How were you shaped and developed spiritually as a young person? This discussion needs to begin with a framework or spiritual scaffolding. For this journey to More, you should consider what has shaped you. Regardless of where you are on your spiritual journey, you have a spiritual framework that was placed within you throughout your developmental years, and the questions above are important ones to ask. Discovering everything God has for you, including the Immeasurably More that He has for you, will be much easier to grasp if we take the time to look at the factors in our life that we have not had control over. Choices were made for us as children that have a tremendous impact on how we view and relate to God the Father, His Son, and Holy Spirit. For this journey, we are going to consider six components that shape us as humans. Perhaps there are others. In order to examine, specifically, spiritual development, let's consider the possibility that, as children, we are placed into one-of-a-kind environments, frameworks that shape us. The six components of bringing up a child can be thought of as the six sides of a cube, the six walls of a box that is designed to guide us as we grow until we reach a maturity where we take the responsibility for our own growth and development.

Just like any cube has six sides, imagine growing and developing within an invisible, metaphoric cube throughout your childhood that essentially made you into who you are today. The six factors listed below shape the life of everyone, but not all have equal weight or impact. The six factors that shape the spiritual development of children are:

1. Family
2. Education
3. Culture
4. Relationships
5. God's Word/The Absence of God's Word
6. Time (specifically eternity).

At first glance, you may dismiss one or more, question how these are to be defined, and/or not recognize the value of one or more, but be sure that each of these six components has either had a great impact on your spiritual development or the lack of them has shaped the way you respond to God.

Beyond the impact that each of these factors has on the spiritual development of an individual, their position within the "cube" of development is also important. Imagine a cube. Label each side of the cube with one of the six components. For example, someone growing up in an American Christian home would likely have family as their base or bottom side, *God's Word*, *relationships*, *education*, and *culture* as the four walls, and *time* as the top or roof. The component with the greatest foundational impact is the component that seems to support all of the others. Any of the six components can be placed in any position. The position of the six components could possibly change or switch positions within one's development, but position is important. You can identify what position each component has had in your own upbringing and make an application accordingly.

For the purposes of investigating the Less we are living in today, imagine yourself standing within your cube of development and facing forward, looking at the *relationship wall* of your cube. Looking above, we will notice that our ceiling is *time (eternity)*. Directly behind us is the wall labeled *family*. On our left is *culture*. On our right is *education*. Beneath our feet is *God's Word*. If you did not grow up in church, much less have the opportunity of an education based on Scripture, then the floor may be hard for you to imagine. Perhaps *family* has been your rock, your foundation. Leave it be for now, and we will return to the role of God's Word, or the lack thereof, in the formation of our spiritual development shortly.

Beyond just standing in this cube of spiritual development, consider yourself a seed planted in the ground. A cube-like scaffolding was/is placed around you. As you grow into a sapling, you are placed in a cube planter with a dirt floor, glass walls, and glass ceiling—a greenhouse. Your life grows by the light that comes through the four glass walls and ceiling, filtered by each of the factors around you: relationships, family, culture, education, and time.

Regardless of which wall is labeled *family*, this one should be easiest to identify and understand its impact. Let's begin here to build our spiritual development cube. We all require other humans to care for us in infancy and childhood. There is no difference for spiritual development. Those who care for us may or may not be biologically related to us, but if they have cared for us and provided our "upbringing," then we refer to them as family. Family contributes greatly to every aspect of our development, and our spiritual development is no exception. We are shaped by those who feed us, bathe us, rock us to sleep, read to us, play with us, converse with us, and physically touch us from the moment we are born and, to some extent, even before we are born. A child will not survive if left on their own at birth. We need others to live. Whether they or we realize it, anyone helping care for an infant and young child on a regular basis is leaving an imprint on their life and is helping shape who they will be. This factor is huge in the life of everyone, unlike culture, education, and God's Word that have varying impact depth depending on the individual. The "family factor" also has an impact on the other five factors. The "family factor" is a load-bearing wall of sorts. Determining the extent of its impact on any given life may be impossible without extensive investigation.

The "education factor" may be the easiest to identify in spiritual development. A few simple questions will provide a great amount of insight into the impact on one's life. Were you formally educated? Where did you go to school? Did you go to a public, private school, or were you homeschooled? Do you have a secondary education? Higher education? These provide plenty of information to assess the impact of education on one's spiritual development. However, a few additional questions will likely explain nuances and particulars, possibly shedding much light on how one relates to God, Christ, and specifically Holy Spirit. This is true in my own story. Perhaps you should consider your individual teachers and how they were educated or their worldview perspectives. You may even want to consider educational trends that were common throughout your school years. The fact that I went to a Baptist Christian elementary and middle school, contrasted with a public high school in North Carolina, and followed by a liberal arts university, definitely impacted my own journey.

One of the most obvious differences I noticed between my husband's and my spiritual mindsets and worldviews was when I was dating him and early in marriage; they seemed to stem from the fact that I attended a private Christian elementary and middle school. He was educated in a public school during his entire education. This was not a black-and-white kind of difference, but subtle differences in our approach to life and interpretation of the world around us and our interpretation of Scripture, even though, for all intents and purposes, we lived in the same world. The way in which we are educated as children undeniably contributes to this cube that we grow up in and that shapes our life, our worldview, and how we interact with the world around us. The differences may be subtle on the exterior, but their impact carries much greater weight. The fact that my teachers at a Christian elementary school approached history, science, and social studies in light of Scripture, they required me to memorize scripture verses, they taught me stories from the Bible, and I attended a weekly chapel service—essentially was a church service for children—I was spiritually molded to a different depth than my peers in public school. When considering how my education was the third wall, so to speak, of the cube I grew up in, this wall has not been cut in any prefabricated way. This wall was hand cut in that my education was a blend of religious and secular. Beyond that, my educational experience is, undoubtedly, as equally unique as my fingerprint, for I can guarantee that no other child on the planet has experienced the same combination of teachers in the same order as I have. My educational experience is one of a kind. Adding my college and graduate school experiences would give an even greater defense of this position. From the sweetest ever first-grade teacher on the planet to the meanest third-grade teacher, the most secular tenth-grade biology teacher pounding the theory of evolution in my head, the most high-maintenance geometry teacher, a meticulously thorough eleventh-grade world history teacher, a bizarre linguistics professor and a nearly-blind introduction to film professor; surely no one else on the planet experienced the thread of formalized education that I did. Surely, no one on the planet has the same perspective. No one on the planet has the same perspective that you do, either. My education has certainly shaped me. Yours has shaped you. As we age, we realize how much we do not know, and as an adult, we are most often resigned to self-education. Once this decision is made, the wall of education no longer will restrict your thinking, but it will continue to contribute to the framework with which you approach life. Acknowledge the contributions to your worldview and the ability to reason and process all of the input from your world today.

As easy as it may be to identify the "education factor" of spiritual development, the hardest to identify is likely the "culture factor." Culture is a blend of all that our five senses experience in the world around us but is unique to the time and place in which we live. There are still questions we can ask to narrow down the strongest influences, but they certainly are not as concrete. The most obvious questions are: where and when did you grow up? What traditions and customs shaped your day-to-day life? To what degree did books, television, Hollywood, and music impact your life? What toys did you play with as a child? Did you grow up in a city, suburb, or rural community? What was the landscape of home? These questions will scratch the surface for sure, but it is possible that more pointed questions are necessary to uncover the impact of the "culture factor." What were your extra-curricular activities as a child? What was your favorite band? Did you have Hollywood crushes? What movie can you quote from memory? What holidays were the most important to you? How did you celebrate Halloween? Did anyone in your life emphasize the supernatural? Each of these questions can lead to further questions that, like the grooves on a vinyl record, can either produce a melody or irritating scratches depending on how they are played out today. The lines between secular and spiritual culture are blurred. What defines culture to each of us is a tapestry of the spiritual and secular. Our spiritual development does not have to have a component identified as church, but church is greatly impacted by culture, whether we attend on a weekly basis or not. Church culture can have a separate definition all on its own. The way in which someone relates to the church culture that they are most closely connected with greatly impacts their spiritual development. Church culture may or may not have a significant impact on your spiritual development. For the purposes of this discussion, Church culture will be equated to religious beliefs and practices demonstrated by a body of believers that one interacted with on a regular basis during any given period of upbringing.

Whether we are growing or are mature, our relationships shape us. We are obviously most shaped by those who play the biggest roles in our lives: parents, grandparents, caregivers, siblings, aunts, uncles, cousins, friends, teachers, etc. We are impacted and influenced by countless people. We may even be greatly impacted by people that we never ever actually meet. We are impacted by authors, actors, leaders, and athletes. If we have a relationship with Jesus Christ, we are impacted by Him. Specifically, through the mystery of the Holy Trinity of Father, Son, and Holy Spirit, one can be impacted by one Person of the Godhead, two or all three. Once I took my own spiritual development upon myself, I realized that I have a distinct relationship with each Person of the Trinity. This truth is a huge part of my personal Immeasurably More story. If this seems foreign or unlikely to you, I would simply say, "But wait, there's More."

Consider the "relationship factor" to be the fourth wall of your spiritual development cube. This specifically needs to be the fourth wall because we are created to be relational people. We are created to live in community. No man is an island. We are made to communicate, relate, and share. Relationships are what is in front of us. Relationships are what give meaning to each day. The fourth wall is the wall we face. Who do you face on any given day? Are you relating to your spouse today? Your friends? Your parents? Your children? Your co-workers? Some days, it may be a whole slew of people. Other days, you may not relate to anyone, but it is unlikely that if you are reading this book, you have not related to someone recently. Ask how relationships with people in your world are impacting your relationship with Jesus Christ.

Our decision to have a relationship with anyone is personal and one that cannot be made for us. We have to make this decision on our own. However, our spiritual development is very much a community effort. This is true even in the lack of a relationship with God or that of the life of an atheist or agnostic. Community, family, and peer pressure shape us and lead us to a choice of accepting or rejecting God. Consider how your community, your tribe, is pointing you to God or distracting you from seeing His hand at work or hearing His voice. The people we spend the most time with are usually affirming our lifestyle and choices. The choice to pursue the Immeasurably More is ours, but it will either be encouraged or discouraged by those we are in relationship with.

Family, education, culture, and relationships are the four walls of the framework that shapes our spiritual development. They form your cube. They all are dependent on, made up of, and uniquely built by people around us. Consider the people in your life, past and present, and how they are shaping you. Are they? Maybe they are pointing you toward More, but is it the world's more or Christ's Immeasurably More?

Before we determine if we have the framework that we need for discovering our More, we have to consider the foundation and ceiling. Next, we will discuss how God's Word and time impact our spiritual formation. Just as our four walls can have a positive or negative impact on spiritual development, there are two possible influences that God's Word and time can have on us. The difference between the presence or absence of God's Word will determine the impact of the foundation of your spiritual development. The impact of time, ironically, comes in the recognition of an absence of time or a day to come when there is no more time. The questions that this kind of ceiling raises requires we look closer at our framework.

Chapter 3

"How firm a foundation, O saints of the Lord, is laid for your faith in His excellent Word" (George Keith). Indeed. Any of you who grew up in a traditional protestant church will likely know this song. Those of you who are unfamiliar with this lyric are welcome to take this statement at face value, even if you do not consider yourself a saint. God's written Word, compiled as the Bible, is absolutely, positively the strongest foundation for any life. Is it the foundation for your life? God's Word is true. God's Word is reliable. God's Word has been tested time and time again and has been found to be all that it claims. God's Word is forever settled in heaven (Psalm 119:89). Scripture is the foundation for faith and, for some of us, a foundation for our lives. I cannot think of anything better. As we consider the framework of our lives and, by extension, the framework for our "More," we certainly need to examine our foundation. Let's ask a few questions to determine what the foundation of our life is and then decide if that foundation is strong or weak.

Determining the role that Scripture plays in your framework may be a simple yes or no question. Were you exposed to any Bible teaching or preaching during your years as a child or teenager? If the answer is no, then God's Word will probably be a poorly constructed left or right wall from verses you have seen used in media or by a religious relative. If the answer to that question is yes, then you have to ask yourself questions like: How much Scripture do I have memorized? Did my parents teach me ideas and concepts based on scripture? Did I have actual, living examples of Scripture present in my upbringing? Did I ever study Scripture on my own, have a daily, personal Bible study when I read Scripture and personally prayed to God? Within each of those questions are further questions to uncover the depth of your foundation in Scripture.

Comedian John Crist did a bit called "The Bible Verse Lady." He imitates and exaggerates the behavior of some Christians who apply a scripture verse or passage to nearly every situation. Search "Bible Verse Lady John Crist" on YouTube, and you will hear him say in a shopping mall: "Thirty percent off. Yes, 'all things work together for the good,'" "Uh, no, thank you, I don't need any skincare samples. 'I am fearfully and wonderfully made,'" and "Look at these watches!—'For such a time as this!'" This video is only about ninety seconds long, but John has about eighteen or so misapplied scriptures. The bit is hilarious because of his perfectly timed delivery and the character he has created. However, the underlying truth, or hard pill to swallow, that he has wrapped up so hilariously is that many of us, Christians or not, know a handful or more of Scripture verses that have framed our lives. I would ask you, though, to take a moment and consider whether they are your framework, a firm foundation, or a faux pas in your life.

John Crist seems to have tweaked real-life scenarios to over-accentuate the absurdity of those who have a Bible verse to apply to every situation. *The Bible Verse Lady* is one of my all-time favorite bits by him because I have heard the same scriptures used by pompous, prideful Christian women and men all throughout my life. I have also thought of those verses in my own mind in situations such as he depicts. This would not be so relatable to me had I not grown up with Scripture as a regular part of my life and been in church every time the doors were open. I heard scripture like Philippians 4:13, Jeremiah 29:11, Romans 8:28 quoted, read them on cross-stitch samplers, plaques, attended a minimum of three church services a week, attended Christian school through the eighth grade where I was required to memorize Scripture and was given many other miscellaneous opportunities to be exposed to Scripture. I have the verses permanently etched on my brain. With a little more focus and effort, I could be "The Bible Verse Lady." Do I want to be? Yes and no. I want to know Scripture so well that it comes to mind in every situation, but I certainly don't want to be known for the misapplication or using it to condemn others. I pray that my pride does not grow to be so great that I become blind to my verbally using God's Word as a proverbial club to beat others down. However, having an arsenal of the very words of God within my mind comes with very real power to overcome temptations and difficult circumstances and to access godly wisdom. Many of the same scriptures that I have spoken or have been spoken to me in condescending tones to embarrass, shame, or try to convict in struggles of sin are a foundation and rock for me to navigate this scary, uncertain world and represent promises that a personal Lord and Savior gives to assure we are not alone. They remind us that He is omnipotent, omniscient, and omnipresent.

In a later chapter, we will discuss how Jesus is the Way, the Truth, and the Life, which comes from scripture in John 14:6. These seven words are a great example of how something so finite in graphite can represent a deep well of knowledge that can engage all of your senses. Just as the foundation of a house may be represented by a simple line on one page of the architect's blueprints, further study will show that even a slab foundation is more than a thin layer of concrete. A better question may be, "How firm is your foundation?"

If God's Word is not your foundation, then it is likely to be relationships, education, or family. Having a foundation of culture is unlikely for anyone simply because culture changes so much so quickly. When we discuss eternity in the coming pages, I will make the case that it can only ever be our ceiling. How could you have a foundation of something that does not exist yet? Relationships, education, or family could easily be your foundation. Which of these was a great emphasis placed on by your parents? Do you have wall decor that says, "Family Is Everything," hanging in your living room? Whenever a problem arises, do you call your dad or grandma first? Are you often given the advice to call Uncle So-and-So and see what he has to say about the situation because he has a Ph.D. in something? Maybe your foundation is your own education. Did you go to a private prep school? Did you have a full ride to the most prestigious college in your home state? Were your parents the ones who hounded you to get good grades? Was there ever even the slightest possibility that you wouldn't attend a four-year secondary school and get a degree in something? How important is education to you? Was education placed with such importance in your family that you rely on your knowledge and intellect as a foundation for your personal worldview?

Could your foundation be one, two, or three key relationships in your life? Who is the "rock" in your life? Who has had such a role in shaping you that it is nearly impossible to separate your life from theirs? Could there be a person whose influence on your life has been so great that their own personal beliefs and convictions are the foundation for your spiritual development? Your mom could be your foundation. Your papa could be your foundation. Jesus could be your foundation. It is possible to have Jesus be your foundation without having a working knowledge of Scripture. As with any of the five possible types of foundation for your spiritual development and framework, once determined, you must investigate further to identify the depth to which that foundation goes.

For the Sunday school-raised readers, this is where we insert a reminder of the parable of the house built on the rock:

> Everyone who hears my teaching and applies it to his life can be compared to a wise man who built his house on an unshakable foundation. When

the rains fell and the flood came, with fierce winds beating upon his house, it stood firm because of its strong foundation. But everyone who hears my teaching and does not apply it to his life can be compared to a foolish man who built his house on sand. When it rained and rained and the flood came, with wind and waves beating upon his house, it collapsed and was swept away.

Matthew 7:24–29 (TPT)

Before you can experience the More that God has in store for you, you must consider and determine your foundation. Without a foundation on the Word of God, you can experience More, but not Immeasurably More. More apart from the Way, the Truth, and the Life will only satisfy temporarily. A foundation on a relationship, on your education, or family may give you security for a season or seasons, but not all seasons of life. Foundations built on people and knowledge always have holes in them because there are no perfect people, and imperfect people cannot teach you the whole truth. God's Word is the whole Truth, and He is the embodiment of perfection. He is your firm foundation.

Chapter 4

What is your ceiling? Do you have one? What is it made of? Are ceilings or roofs a part of the framework of your spiritual development? Maybe you do not have one. Perhaps yours is made of glass. Mine was for most of my life. A glass ceiling can give the appearance of no ceiling but brings great restraint when tested. It can stunt your growth. It keeps you small. Your ceiling will keep you from reaching your potential.

Most people seem to have a glass ceiling on their cube of spiritual development. This glass ceiling prevents the ability to live daily life with an eternal perspective. There is something like a tangible reality of 85–95 years. This, of course, is far too often interrupted by a friend or loved one who is "lost too soon" to an accident or illness. Regardless of a specific number of years or other life expectancy factors, most people, especially in the USA, see life as finite and have a number range that they generally associate with life. Eternity is a separate concept from life here and now.

Perhaps your ceiling is clouded. Maybe your ceiling is dark, black, or just bleak. Have you ever considered the ceiling of your life? Without hope, you may be avoiding the thought and idea of the ceiling of your life. You may never stop to consider what is beyond.

Are you a "believer" in Jesus Christ? Your ceiling may have light streaming in. Light may be streaming in, but your ceiling is definitely intact, with reality completely contained within the cube. You live life with little acknowledgment or thought, even of eternity. This is especially true of believers in the American church. You likely do not recognize the impact that decisions made on Earth and within our cube are having on eternity through our choices and prayers. As we talk about our life in Christ, lead others to Scripture, and maybe even introduce others to eternal salvation in Jesus Christ and the idea of eternal life, we are engaging with angelic and demonic beings that are waging war in the spiritual realm. We do not acknowledge these beings because either we fear what we don't know, we fear demonic involvement in our lives, or we are ignorant of such things.

Everyone has a "ceiling," whether acknowledged or not, until such time that they break through it and embrace eternity. Embracing eternity is part of the Immeasurably More that can be discovered. Embracing eternity will impact your worldview, daily outlook, and every relationship that you have. Embracing eternity brings awareness to how everything we say and do on Earth is charting a trajectory for our lives. Living in less limits our view of eternity. Living in less only allows us to see life through the perspective of 85–95 years. "Your fleeting life is but a warm breath of air that is visible in the cold only for a moment and then it vanishes" (James 4:14b, TPT).

Throughout this book, scriptures will be mentioned, like the one above and the Matthew 7 reference from before, which are familiar to many Christians. There is an obvious connection to the subject at hand, but ask yourself if you see More. Are you thinking, "I get it. Heaven is forever and now is not. The days are long, but the years are short. Next time I blink, my eight-year-old will be eighteen." But wait, I tell you, there's More. There is a greater depth to this. Once you discover More, part of everything you never knew you always wanted will be an outlook on life that is convinced that today, even though I can count its seconds, is part of an eternal, never-ending story. Investing in eternity is just as much a part of your day as is fulfilling obligations to family, job, and community. Receiving Holy Spirit allows us to invest in eternity. Just like depositing funds into the bank, we can access elements of eternity while we are still on Earth. We can access God's glory, His presence, His peace, and wisdom. Eternity does not have to be something that we get to one day. Eternity began for me in May 1981. At that time, I began investing in eternity, but sadly, I did not begin withdrawing the More that Holy Spirit offers until December 2018. I am discovering that, unlike my earthly bank account, my eternal account is compounding interest and will never, ever run out. There are riches untold stored up for me. I can access them now and every moment for the remainder of eternity. We cannot access these riches, though, if we find ourselves stuck in a moment that has passed us by already. We can become stuck in moments of happier days, memories of our younger selves, or younger children; we can get stuck in regret and fear.

A recent discovery of an aspect of More has been in a rejection of the idea that time is a thief. Perhaps with the access to thousands upon thousands of images from the past 15–20 years in digital form, we are tempted to sit in the past rather than embrace the present and look with hope to the future. Sadness overcomes us as we long for days gone by. "Facebook memories" remind us of what we had that is gone now. I keep hearing women, especially, say, "Time is a thief," or posting it on their social media accounts. I noticed that most of the women saying this are the ones whose children were born and raised since digital pictures became accessible to the general public. I cannot help but wonder if the technological development of our pixelated histories is tying us to the past, holding us in the memories, and tempting us to buy the lie that then is better than now and that which is yet to come. We speak and sing of better days yet to come, but maybe our culture does not actually believe this idea. As we continue to discover More and let go of Less in our life, we will be able to identify this lie that something was stolen from us or is being stolen from us.

Our enemy is a thief, but time is not. Time is a gift because all we are promised is right now, today. Today will not be stolen from us if we lay it back down at the feet of Jesus, commit it to Him, and strive to live for Him in every moment. He will give us moments, memories, experiences that are incomparable to others, and the memories of those will become cherished gems in our minds.

Chapter 5

Let's do some unpacking. Imagine your cube. This cube represents your life and what has shaped you. Identifying the six sides of the cube will reveal all of the factors that have influenced your life and guided your path. Our paths are guided by knowledge, words, light, sound, and possibly even tastes and smells—all of your senses and experiences are, have, and will contribute to who you are and will become. As you identify these factors and influences, ask how the following walls of your own, individual, "one-of-a-kind because there is no other you cube" have brought you to where you are today spiritually. Taking this type of inventory of your life could be the key to unlocking the More and discovering everything you never knew you always wanted in Christ because we move toward More when we ask questions and seek answers to what God has in store for our lives.

Questions are grossly underrated, especially in one's spiritual development. Some leaders of churches even discourage the asking of questions. Perhaps you were never encouraged to ask questions. Perhaps you were never even allowed to ask questions of the worldview that was offered to you, either from culture, your education, your family, or the church you attended.

As you unpack boxes after a move, or those of Christmas decorations, or if you have the weighty challenge of unpacking the belongings of a loved one who has passed away, memories rise to the surface of your mind, but often there are questions in tow. Where did this come from? Who did this belong to? Why do we still have this? How has this survived? These are all questions that could apply to any of the above scenarios but that we should also use to take inventory of our relationship with Jesus Christ.

Take a few minutes to ask and consider these questions… The goal is to discover More. More is always more than this. This is whatever you have, believe, or know right now. Take some time to examine your cube and ask these questions:

1. What is the foundation of your life? What is the floor of your cube? Who or what is or has been your rock in life?

2. What are the walls that guide you as you face life and relationships? If you were standing in this imaginary cube of life, what wall do you reach out and touch on your right side? Which one is on your left?

3. What wall is behind you? What aspect of your life has been there for you to lean upon? What aspect of your life has had your back in life's most difficult seasons?

4. What is out in front of you? What aspect of your life do you interact with the most? What aspect of your life gives you feedback, responds to your words and actions as well as elicits your responses?

5. Look up. What or who do you see? Can you see beyond the four walls of your current life and circumstances? Do you imagine how your choices today will impact you throughout eternity?

"Watch over your heart with all diligence, for from it flow the springs of life" (Proverbs 4:23).

The above questions will help you identify what or who has shaped your heart, your beliefs, the essence of you. The heart, your soul and spirit, is key. How has your heart been molded and shaped? Everyone is molded and shaped by God's Word (or the lack of it), family, culture, education, relationships, and eternity. These are things we did not have control over as young children, but with varying degrees, we gain control over them as we mature. There is a point when we begin to choose what shapes us. Also, at some point, we need to grow beyond the box and start letting the combination of our minds, will, and emotions lead and guide us. Ideally, by the time you reach the maturity to grow beyond the cube or framework, you will be listening to Holy Spirit's voice and leading in your life. Everyone's heart is shaped by these six factors, but not all are shaped evenly, not all of the sides are shaped completely, and some may even be constricted in how they have developed. God's Word, family, culture, education, relationships, and eternity are the six sides of our proverbial cube. The choices made by you and your parents will determine what is the foundation of your cube. The easiest way to mature to a point of surrender and allow the guidance of Holy Spirit is to have God's Word as your foundation, the base of your cube. Relationships are most naturally the front wall, and Eternity is the top or ceiling. For the purpose of our continued discussion, "Family has your back," education will be your left or right wall depending on your non-dominant handedness. Culture will be on the side of your dominant hand because usually, we have more control over the culture we allow into our lives as a child than we do over our education.

"Trust in the Lord with all your heart and lean not on your own understanding. In all your ways acknowledge Him and He shall direct your path" (Proverbs 3:5–6, NKJV).

Who controls who? Is your trust in God? Do you have the reins of your life, or does God? The above is a verse that is quoted *a lot* among churchgoers, but as we progress through this conversation, we will conclude that as my Pastor Jim used to say, "Their walk talks, and their talk talks, but their walk talks louder than their talk talks" and your walk will indicate that your trust is not fully in God, when you do not give Him the proper reverence, or holy fear. We like to say we are trusting in Him fully and not leaning on our own understanding, but rarely is there definitive evidence of this in our lives.

Whether we recognize this or not, we are dependent on others for our foundation and formation as a child. We don't choose what family or culture we are born into. God does. We cannot survive without the other people that God puts into our lives. There is choice, however, woven in, and we begin to make those choices for our lives even before we are completely conscious of the fact that we are forming ourselves. We typically choose our own friends as early as two or three years of age or at least are showing a preference for some over others. We choose the food, healthy or not so much, as soon as given the opportunity. Not giving those vegetables a second or third try is shaping your physical health for life. Choosing video games, books, team sports, or individual sports at a young age all contribute to the healthy or unhealthy lifestyle we create for ourselves. Although the responsibility of our own development begins beyond ourselves and slowly becomes our own responsibility, personal choice is always a factor and is always a part of the process. As we grow mentally and physically, there is a transfer of power into our development. We were never intended to stay in our cube, though. God is calling you to break the fourth wall in front of you, smash the glass ceiling above you, and step into a life of More.

Breaking the fourth wall and smashing the ceiling of the cube you are standing in is a pivotal step in becoming the man or woman that God truly intended for us to be before we were even formed in our mother's womb. In Psalm 139, there is an elaborate description of how much thought, creativity, and care went into God deciding who He originally wanted and wants you to be. The same chapter outlines the relationship that He wants to have with you now, wherever you are on your spiritual journey, and how wonderful His thoughts and plans for you are if you choose His best for your life.

Would you one more time consider your foundation, your three supporting walls, those people who were always before you in significant relationships, and the ceiling above you? Would you consider these walls, foundation, and ceiling of your cube in light of the following:

> God, investigate my life; get all the facts firsthand. I'm an open book to you; even from a distance, you know what I'm thinking. You know when I leave and when I get back; I'm never out of your sight. You know everything I'm going to say before I start the first sentence. I look behind me and you're there, then up ahead and you're there, too—your reassuring presence, coming and going. This is too much, too wonderful—I can't take it all in!
>
> Is there any place I can go to avoid your Spirit? To be out of your sight? If I climb to the sky, you're there! If I go underground, you're there! If I flew on morning's wings to the far western horizon, You'd find me in a minute — you're already there waiting! Then I said to myself, "Oh he even sees me in the dark! At night I'm immersed in the light!" It's a fact: darkness isn't dark to you; night and day, darkness and light, they're all the same to you.
>
> Oh yes, you shaped me first inside, then out; you formed me in my mother's womb. I thank you, High God—you're

breathtaking! Body and soul I am marvelously made! I worship in adoration—what a creation! You know me inside and out, you know every bone in my body; You know exactly how I was made, bit by bit, how I was sculpted from nothing into something. Like an open book, you watched me grow from conception to birth; all the stages of my life were spread out before you, The days of my life all prepared before I'd even lived one day.

Your thoughts—how rare, how beautiful! God, I'll never comprehend them! I couldn't even begin to count them—any more than I could count the sand of the sea. Oh, let me rise in the morning and live always with you! And please, God, do away with wickedness for good! And you murderers—out of here!—all the men and women who belittle you, God, infatuated with cheap god-imitations. See how I hate those who hate you, God, see how I loathe all this godless arrogance; I hate it with pure, unadulterated hatred. Your enemies are my enemies!

Investigate my life, O God, find out everything about me; Cross-examine and test me, get a clear picture of what I'm about; see for yourself whether I've done anything wrong—then guide me on the road to eternal life.

Psalm 139 (MSG)

From this precious paraphrase of the Psalm that provides a foundation for God's love, desires, and good will for each of us—no matter what makes up your cube—I hope you will see that your Creator wants More for you. Your Creator wants more time with you, He wants you to know how important you are to Him, and He wants you to know that He is and will always be there for you.

God knows what you are thinking, so why don't you ask Him what He thinks about your thoughts?

God knows where you are going, so why don't you ask Him what He thinks about where you are going? Maybe He has a better destination in mind.

God knows what you should say in every situation. Why don't you ask Him to give you the words for that difficult conversation you need to have? "And now, O Lord, hear their threats, and give us, your servants, great boldness in speaking your word" (Acts 4:29, NLT).

Sometimes, we question in abundance without asking the right questions. Many times, the most important answers we need are answers to the questions that we aren't even asking. We can ask Him that, too. Lord, what questions do I need to ask of You? Lord, will You show me what I don't know about You? Lord, will You show me more of You? Lord, show me who I am in You. Show me, Lord, who You made me to be. Lord, show me more of me.

Chapter 6

Y ou don't know what you don't know.

I have many smile-giving childhood memories of looking over at my brother, who is three years older, giving him some statement (ranging anywhere on the spectrum between ignorant and brilliant) that was followed with the tagline, "…and now you know." Sometimes, he would be the one making the statement, but without missing a beat, the response of the other would be, "…and knowing is half the battle." This would immediately be followed by a chorus of *G.I. Joe!* This call and response was a staple in our sibling communication throughout the '80s. We watched the *G.I. Joe* cartoon and learned many life lessons (eye roll).

This staple from my childhood, now recalled in adulthood, often reminds me more of what I don't know than what I do know. This begs, pleads, and urges the question: how can we possibly know what we don't know? This has the potential to cause many problems in life, or perhaps "ignorance is bliss." This also provides ground for those who believe they "know-it-all" and allow pride to blind them to the truth that there is More. To have the attitude or presumption that you are an expert on any given subject, even yourself, is to allow pride to blind you to truth. God only knows. Only God knows all there is to know. He is omniscient. Anyone speaking with authority uncoupled with humility is setting themself up for a fall. See Proverbs 16:18.

You can spend your entire childhood and young adulthood knowing that there is more to a story and be perfectly content with the amount of knowledge you have. Sometimes, it would be nice if you could unlearn something, but at least we have the ability to forget sometimes. Often, we know what we know and either believe we know too much or are content that we know just enough. The difference would be between that of a seeker and a non-participant.

All four walls of my own spiritual development cube shaped me to be a lifelong learner, and somewhere along the way, I started asking the question, "What don't I know?" If the right seeds are cultivated, everyone can develop the desire to know what "More" is out there and seek to find it.

You don't know what you don't know, but you can choose to seek out what you don't know.

Are you a "know-it-all," are you blind, are you ignorant, or just not engaging in the pursuit of More? Sometimes truth is hidden. Sometimes More is in front of us but disguised or hidden. Sometimes what we should or need to know has been omitted by those who have shaped us. Sometimes we have spiritual blinders on that we are unaware of.

The Apostle Paul was a "know-it-all." He was a seeker, a student, and probably top of his class. He was described as a student of Gamaliel, a famous Rabbi of his day (Acts 22:3). He knew so much that he had himself convinced that those who did not believe as he did deserved persecution and/or death. Paul is often put on a pedestal for his teaching; he is honored and revered, but not of his own making. Many of us put him and the other authors of Scripture in a place in our minds where we can't relate to them fully. They are kind of "altogether other." I am guilty of this. When I read of the horrible things that Paul did, I separate myself from them. When I think of what he endured after he met Jesus face to face and his efforts to see the good news of the Kingdom of God spread throughout the world, in my mind, I do not place myself on the same playing field as Paul. What if I did? Perhaps I could let go of pride that separates me from others who don't know what I know, those who may know more about a subject than I do, or those who are stuck in the belief of "the Jesus I know right now is enough."

Some of the greatest advice to take in the pursuit of More is that which was given to me from long before I can remember... Seeds that were planted in my mind as an infant or toddler in a small church in Kernersville, NC. Perhaps the same seed was planted in your mind in the lyrics of a familiar hymn. "Turn your eyes upon Jesus. Look full in His wonderful face, and the things of Earth will grow strangely dim in the light of His glory and grace" (Helen H. Lemmel).

How blind are you? How well can you focus on what is in front of you? How is your peripheral vision? Perhaps what you don't know about the More that Jesus offers is simply not in focus. Perhaps you need a little magnification. Step closer to Jesus. He will reveal to you everything you didn't know you wanted to know, and so much more. Perhaps the world, loved ones, idols, or various other distractions have grabbed your attention. While you can give me baseball statistics, the names of every pop radio hit this year, or all the health benefits of a cold plunge, you may not be able to tell me how to experience the manifest presence of Holy Spirit. If you ask Holy Spirit, He will show you how to experience His presence. Just ask. Wait until you hear from Him. He will speak when your heart is quiet enough to hear him.

"You do not have because you do not ask" (James 4:2b, NASB).

"Draw near to God and He will draw near to you" (James 4:8, NASB).

But wait, there's More. There is more that God wants you to know. God wants you to know His glory, His presence, His peace, Kingdom, and wisdom. God wants you to know that you can be rich in Christ. He wants you to know that you have greater levels of freedom that you have yet to access. He wants you to know that you are being lied to by many people around you who influence you. He wants you to know truth. He wants you to know that you can be delivered from that which holds you in bondage. He wants you to know that there are greater depths of love, grace, and mercy that you have yet to tap into. He wants you to know that there is abundance waiting for you. He wants you to know of the things that you are letting pass you by because you have been trained to think, *That is too good to be true.* In Christ, there is nothing that is too good to be true. You may not understand what, how, or why that blows your mind, but if He is behind it, it is possible. Anything is possible in Christ. Your Heavenly Father wants you to know that so much of what your heart truly desires is not dependent on you. Holy Spirit wants you to recognize that you have made many partnerships with our enemy, Satan, and that you continue to walk in defeat partnered with him when you could be walking in the joy of freedom. If you are a control freak, Jesus wants you to let Him control your "freakin'" self. God wants you to ask yourself if you are being a tyrant within your own life. For those of us who find ourselves in church every Sunday, our good, good Father is asking us to consider how much of the other six days of the week we are giving over to the bad, bad father.

Ask yourself if you know, or could even define, the glory of God. Have you experienced the manifest presence of God? Have you met Him in such a profoundly personal way that you are now completely different? Have you been transformed in such a way that can only be explained by having met Jesus? Consider the apostle Paul's story. Do you have a similar one? God's peace may be something you know a little about and have experienced in a specific way, but wait, there's More. Have you experienced the peace of God to the extent that you are unshakeable when you receive devastating news? Do you realize that when you recite the familiar "Lord's Prayer" from Matthew 6, it is possible to experience His "Kingdom come" in a tangible way? The Kingdom of God is here now (Matthew 4:17) and is not just something to be realized in eternity. Do you realize that Wisdom is a person you can have a relationship with? Do you realize that God longs to give you more wisdom in the person of Holy Spirit? There's More, I tell you. Seek to know Jesus more. To know Him is to want to know Him more. Do you really know Jesus? Do you really want to know Jesus more? If your answer is "yes," seek Him. The remaining chapters of this book should help you do so. If your answer is "no," then there probably is not anything else for you within these pages. If your answer is "yes, but…," then hang on.

Chapter 7

More would be great. Who doesn't want more blessing, favor, answered prayer, wisdom, knowledge, peace, mercy, and grace? More sounds wonderful, but… Is there a hesitant thought in your mind? Is there a glitch? Are you having a hard time envisioning more? Are you unsure? Are you tangled up in the here and now? Are you reluctant to consider what could be because of what currently is?

Perhaps you are thinking that in order to get more from God, you will have to do more. Certainly, More means more work, more time, more study, more service, and more concentration. Right? To discover the More that God has for you will require more time. You may be thinking, "I don't have any time to give." This all sounds great, but you couldn't possibly add another thing to your schedule, and you know if you set your alarm clock 15–30 minutes earlier, that you will just hit snooze.

More does require time, but it does not have to be scheduled. The time that it takes to find More in Christ is made up of focus and intention rather than minutes and seconds.

"Draw near to God and He will draw near to you" (James 4:8, NKJV).

Our Father in Heaven, our Savior at His side, and Holy Spirit are all waiting to meet you wherever you are for whatever amount of time you offer them. Draw near to God, and He will draw near to you. You go first. You step first. Turn your eyes upon Jesus. All of the verbs imply that you choose, in your free will, to step toward Him. He will meet you in any moment, at any place. "Yes, but… I tried that. Nothing happened." Pursuing More means that we have to identify the Less that we are living in right now before we can recognize the More He is offering. Let's put a pin in that. We will revisit the Less shortly.

Yes, but…

More does require an investment, but there is no minimum investment. More does require time, but we all have time that doesn't really get counted in our day because we are on autopilot. God will use literally any amount of time that you will give Him and will give you More in return, with compound interest. You can learn to insert worship and study into already-established routines and meet with Him in the midst of the mundane.

More requires a withdrawal as well. More of Him requires withdrawal from self. More requires stepping away from the Less we are living in. This Less we are living in sounds minimal, considering the very nature of the language we must use to uncover it, but the Less we need to discuss has consumed us. The Less we are living in is a result of the weeds of the world that have us trapped, entangled, and tripping over ourselves within the cube of our spiritual development. More requires breaking the fourth wall and smashing the dim glass ceiling of our cube in order to step out of those weeds.

Back to the cube. The cube is a dark place without the Light of Jesus Christ. The cube, even if constructed on a foundation of God's Word, with a Christian family raising you in church, attending a Christian Elementary School, and living in the "buckle" of the Bible Belt, even with the "perfect" construction, formula, recipe and ingredients is dreadfully dark, broken, full of cracks, and was never meant to be a place to truly live or thrive. Your cube is meant to be a framework for growing you to a moment of choice. Everyone must choose whether or not to stay in their cube or break out of it to grow in the light of God's glorious grace. Trees are placed in green houses in order to build a strong root system and trunk. They are not meant to live their entire lives within a green house.

Chapter 8

The Black Box Theater is a versatile performance space. Community theater troupes will often paint the walls of a large room black, hang some black curtains over doorways, add some lighting, and line up a few rows of chairs in order to convert a space once used as a cafeteria, conference room, or even storefront into their stage with now limitless possibilities. Although there may be limits to the size of the cast, audience, and live musicians, the black box theater has no limitations on the impact that can be made by the performers on their audience. Consider who your audience is.

Though a dark room, the black box theater allows for life to shine. The theater puts a spotlight on and shares life through stories of unlikely heroes and heroines. Stories are told of the underdog, the overcomer, and those stepping into destiny. Entering the black box theater is like looking at a blank canvas, and then, within moments, a beautiful story through living pictures emerges as if Bob Ross himself walked into the room. The black box theater allows for the mingling, sharing, and giving of life among the players and the audience. The beauty of faces, words, gestures, movement, set design, choreography, and so much more is woven together in a matter of moments. It is magical how walking into a room which, at first glance, is dark and limiting is discovered to contain such abundant life and such possibility. How can such beauty and abundant life be bound in darkness, enclosed in all black? The darkness limits our ability to see the source of life.

Our personal cube has quite the metaphoric resemblance. Our foundation, walls, and ceiling are all masked in black because of the sin nature that we were born into, constructed as a framework for our life from the beginning of time. "There is nobody living right, not even one…" (Romans 3:10, MSG). We try. Our parents tried to "raise us right." Most sought to bring us life-giving relationships and opportunities. Living in a sin-cursed world, the dark is comfortable, actually. Darkness is more comfortable than light, sometimes, because of our origin story. Because the original humans chose darkness over light, every single one of us grows up on the stage of a black box theater. Our stage, whether it is God's Word, family, education, culture, or relationships, is surrounded by darkness and separation from God. We trip across it because we were taught wrong, we were disappointed, important lessons were omitted, we missed that day, we were led astray, we were deceived. We can put on our best performance, but we didn't set the stage ourselves. We didn't place the markers; the bad, bad father did. Directors and stage managers can make you or break you in a performance. In life, your director in the darkness is a liar whose singular focus is to steal the spotlight, kill the lights on your best scene, and destroy the sets of others, like your parents, who spent so much time designing. Your stage manager is one or more of the bad father's minions following his manifesto of "steal, kill, destroy" (John 10:10).

Family, culture, education, and relationships have shaped us. Since they are at the mercy of this ruthless bad father, the director we get by default, our walls are full of cracks, our stage is uneven, our curtains are unraveling, and the lights have been left unfocused. Examining this black box that we have grown up in and been formed in reveals that the ground, the stage, is actually cluttered with broken props, former costumes strewn about, and worn-out furniture that has been misused or overused. We cannot walk from stage right to stage left, upstage or down without stumbling or tripping. The manipulative director is a master at lighting. He keeps the lights low. Imagine how candles and torches reflecting off of shiny metal pieces were used in the earliest days of the theater. Artificial lights are one of his specialties. He illuminates our faults. He illuminates difficult circumstances and relationships. The lights that are focused highlight the purposeless paths and just the exact distraction for the moment that will lead you to act out his story of Less.

While we have a manipulative, evil director and can hardly avoid his stage managers, the performance is still ours to control. Whether or not we hit our marks, deliver our lines, and project our voice appropriately is still all on us. We can fire the director and hire a new one. We can turn on and focus the right lights. We can bring in a new stage manager to clean things up for us, repair the broken, and reset the stage for Act 2. No matter what Act you find yourself in, there is always another or at least an epilogue. God the Father has purchased your stage if you will recognize Him as the owner. He wants to be the investor in your show. Jesus Christ is longing to be your director. He is best suited for the job. Jesus is one of us. He put on the only ever-perfect performance on Earth and has the best experience for the job. Will you let Holy Spirit be your stage manager? He knows how to set the stage perfectly in order to tell your story. He knows which props you need and what to get rid of that is upstaging you now.

So many choices have to be made in order to trade the abysmal summer stock ill-prepared performance for the award-winning all-time-greatest longest-running Broadway hit. Will you recognize the true owner of your black box theater? Which director will you choose? Will you attempt to have co-directors? Who will you trust for lighting, props, and set design? Will you rely on the costumes and props from storage, or will you trade them for the new ones that the Owner offers? Will you allow the true stage manager to do His job, or will you invite the old ones to hang around and give their input?

What about the fourth wall? Are you willing to break the

fourth wall? Your willingness to break the fourth wall is actually what will determine the success of your personal theater and stage.

The most obvious difference between the two directors that you get to choose for the performance of your life is the presence or absence of "the fourth wall." The fourth wall is a concept in modern history of the theater, referring to an imaginary wall between the actors and audience rather than the actual fourth physical wall of whatever building houses the theater. The fourth wall is represented in television, film, and social media by the physical screen separating you from what is being played out, performed, or depicted. The audience does not communicate with the actors because of the fourth wall. The audience does not change the outcome or rewrite the script because of the understood fourth wall. Whether the stage is raised off of the ground and has a visible edge or whether it ends at a line of masking tape on the floor, the audience understands that is where the imaginary wall exists. The fourth wall is a fascinating concept simply because of the impact that it has on any given performance. Despite the wall, the audience is obviously impacted by what happens on stage. The evidence is the laughter, groans, sighs, and applause. Despite the wall, the stage is obviously impacted by the response given by the audience. The actors on stage "feed" off of the positive and negative energy expressed by the audience. There is a symbiotic relationship created by or despite the fourth wall.

"Breaking the fourth wall" most often happens when eye contact is made between those on stage and those in the audience. The fourth wall is broken when the audience shouts out something, and a response is given from the stage. The fourth wall is broken in a lot of ways, but two of the most iconic examples of the fourth wall being broken are, first, the cast members of the TV show *The Office* looking to the camera to give an eye roll or smirk and, secondly, the character Ferris

Bueller as played by Matthew Broderick. Ferris Bueller, in the movie *Ferris Bueller's Day Off*, not only looked directly at the camera but talked to us in the audience—a responsibility given singularly to his character in the film.

Chapter 9

Some things in life are meant to be broken. The proverbial fourth wall of one's life should be broken. The metaphor of the black box theater as life illustrates the spiritual reality: we are cut off from a Good Father by an imaginary, though intensely impactful, fourth wall that was put in place by a bad father who we allow to control all of the properties and atmosphere for what should be our greatest, most-stunning performance—walking in the fullness of who and what our Creator designed us for.

We have no control over the fact that we were raised in our particular cube—not to be confused with having been raised in a barn, as my mother used to imply of me. A common excuse given by the confused, disillusioned, and uneducated is, "I was born this way." This excuse is often misapplied when the sentiment that should be expressed is, "I was raised this way." The cube of our lives has such huge implications that are completely out of our control. We have no control as to which family we are born into, what city we are raised in, what elementary school we first attend, and so on. We have no real control over the first time we are exposed to love, music, television, books, theater, painting, sculpting, gardening, basketball, hunting, and the like before an age when we can express independence in seeking those things out. The same is true of the Good Father. Our exposure to Him, His unbelievable love, and His amazing Kingdom is out of our control. The bad father gets to direct our lives until the fourth wall is broken. The direction of the Good Father will hopefully override the destructive plans of the bad one.

Are there cracks in your walls? The cracks could be broken relationships, unfulfilled dreams, or failed plans. Does light sneak in? Just like when the poorly timed opening of a door floods the black box theater with light and distracts the audience from what is happening on stage, Jesus wants to shine light in on you, put the spotlight on who He made you to be rather than what is broken, askew, and tripping you up.

We are comfortable in our box. The black box theater fosters an intimate experience of entertainment, education, expression, and self-discovery. In our own black box theater, we are in control, or at least we think we are. In the black box, we can focus on those we allow to be close to us, those who we share the stage with. We have a false sense of control in the box, our cube. The director and stage manager remain in the shadows, and it is easy to forget how we are being manipulated, robbed, cheated, and deceived. Out of sight and out of mind are the darker forces at work. Whether or not the spotlight is on us, we focus on what is in the light rather than what is beyond the walls. The lights are usually dim, and much is masked. As long as we are telling our story, we can forget about what is beyond the walls. Control and darkness create a safe, predictable space where we do not have to face the question of eternity and what happens when the show is over and the applause ends.

From the dim lights above to the light coming in from the cracks to the poorly focused stage lighting, you may not be able to clearly see what is right in front of you—your audience. When a performance has a specified lighting design, illumination is intended specifically to enhance the performers and keep what is beyond the fourth wall in the dark. Sometimes, even when on the edge of the stage, what is beyond does not come into focus because of the darkness. Relationships are what is in front of us beyond the fourth wall. The fourth wall is the wall we face. We see through it, but rarely in a performance can anyone make out the individual or individuals comprising what we know to be the audience.

You can know who is in the audience without knowing the audience. You can hear laughter, cheers, applause, sighs, groans, and maybe even heckling from the audience and not know who or how many are out there. Perhaps it is a private performance, by invitation only, with a guest list including the names of each person sitting beyond that fourth wall, but you remain separated from them. Either you know their names but nothing else, or you can't see them and are as clueless about who you are performing for as if all of the house lights were on.

Do you have a relationship with the audience? Is your mom watching? Your spouse? Your friend? Your co-worker? Your neighbor? If the fourth wall remains intact, it doesn't matter who is beyond it; there is no interaction, only an exchange of responses.

Regardless of which director you entrust with the script of your life, your Good Father is watching in delight as you express all of your talents, emotions, and gifts of character. He is waiting for you to break the fourth wall, reach out to Him, connect with Him, engage with Him, and find out the script, stage notes, set design, lighting, and props that He has planned for you.

When we break the fourth wall with an audience, intimacy begins, inside jokes develop, and a shared experience unfolds. The same is true in the metaphor. Bring the fourth wall down and find intimacy with the Good Father, His Son, and His Spirit.

Are you willing to be vulnerable? Are you willing to invite the audience into your story? Are you willing to exchange what you have always known and are comfortable with for the unknown and More? Your Good, Good Father, waiting in the audience, has more in store for you. He wants you to know that He has bigger roles that He wants you to play. He wants you to know that He has a bigger stage that He wants you to shine from. He wants you to know that He has more elaborate costumes for you to wear. He wants you to know that He wants you performing on the stage of an amphitheater where the seating capacity is limitless. He wants you to know that He is your biggest fan. He is smiling and singing over you. There's More, I tell you, there's more He has in store for you.

A choice must be made. Choose today whom you will serve (Joshua 24:15). If you choose the same director and stage managers you have always had, do nothing. Keep on keeping on. If you want to switch directors, call out to Jesus. Surrender your stage and theater to Him.

Chapter 10

Friend, if you are the believer I intended to write for, you do not need to hear another salvation message about choosing Jesus. If by chance you are still confused about who Jesus is and what the Gospel is, please, put this book down for a bit and start reading the book of John in the Bible, a chapter a day, over and over, until you understand the reason Jesus Christ came to Earth. If you need confession for your soul, read Psalm 51 in the Message paraphrase. This is a different message. This is a challenge to make an exchange. Now is the time to trade in the Less you are living in for More. Now is the time to level up. Are you prepared to give up the Less you are living in for the More that God wants to give you? This is not as easy as it may seem. The stage you are currently performing on within your cube is likely all you have ever known, and change is hard. Change means doing things differently, hearing, seeing, and feeling things differently. Walking in newness of life means reacting differently, accepting differently, and ultimately choosing differently. Are you willing to exchange the elephant in the room for the unicorn? The natural for the supernatural? Will you be transformed and have your mind renewed?

An exchange must be made. Many seem to believe that if they work hard enough, then what they have will become More. It may, but it will never be Immeasurably More. More, on our own and in our own strength, will still be calculable, will still be containable, will still be manageable. When the Good Father steps in Immeasurably More (what you never even considered to be a possibility; it is beyond your capabilities), the outcome will be immeasurable or impossible to calculate.

We need to discuss how we can spend days, months, years, and decades in the goodness of God and never realize the greatness of God. We sing of His goodness in church, and we use all of the best words and phrases, but we barely scratch the surface of personal experience with that of which we sing. Think about the difference between being on the winning team of the Super Bowl, World Series, Stanley Cup, or World Cup and receiving the ring in comparison to being in the stands on the day the game was played. Some of us are blown away even by watching the event on TV to the extent that we feel like winners, too, when our favorite team gets the trophy. There's no real comparison, though. Wouldn't you rather have the ring than just know of someone who does? We need to consider the ways in which the framework of our spiritual development allows us to experience God's blessing, His grace, His mercy, and joy, but never His favor, His anointing, or His true supernatural power.

Salvation in Jesus Christ is a one-time choice of believing in Jesus Christ as your Savior and the gospel, or good news of His death, burial, resurrection, and soon return. But wait, there's More. No, you don't have to be more, do more, or give more. Examine your heart for repentance. More comes through the transformation of repentance and choosing Jesus Christ to be Lord, Master, and Director of your life. Be transformed by the renewing of your mind and allow Holy Spirit to work in and through your life to be More for you; allow Holy Spirit to do more for you, and allow Him to give you more and more and more than you ever dreamed of.

Accepting Christ as your Savior metaphorically gives you a ticket to eternity in heaven after physical death. Now is the time to exchange that ticket for heaven on Earth. Eternity can begin today. Your rewards and the supernatural can begin today when you decide to make Him Lord of your life. Many in the church profess Jesus to be their Savior and Lord, but their lives reveal they have the reigns. The heart and life of a believer in Jesus Christ who experiences More is one that does not allow sin to remain.

"No one can serve two masters; for either he will hate the one and love the other, or he will be devoted to one and despise the other. You cannot serve God and wealth" (Matthew 6:24).

Many contemporary Bible teachers have given the illustration of our relationship with God being like a marriage relationship (we are the Bride of Christ, after all). How many husbands are okay with their wives continuing to date their previous boyfriends after they say, "I do"? Christ, the Groom, expects us to give up all of the people and things that take our attention away from Him when we say, "I do." A Holy God cannot tolerate sin or that which separates us from Him. Being married to someone who continues lying, cheating, and stealing is so destructive to the relationship. Our Good Father will not tolerate the habits we bring with us from our previous life with the bad father. Our Good Father will never turn us away, will never deny us, and will continue to pour out His love and blessing on us once we choose Him. However, He reserves the Immeasurably More for those who truly repent, turn from their wicked ways, and allow themselves to be transformed by the renewing of their mind. Salvation gives us the power of being a new creation in Christ. Many professing believers in Jesus Christ have access to the New Man and the Mind of Christ but choose to remain as they were, trying in their own strength to "fix" the old man through willpower instead of the power of Holy Spirit.

Just a few weeks before my fifth birthday, well over forty years ago, I remember sitting at our dining room table and praying a prayer, asking Jesus to be my Savior. I did not experience Immeasurably More until I was forty-two and beyond. Why? Jesus Christ had His rightful place in my heart; I spent years studying the Bible and was a mostly "good girl." I allowed several sins to go unchecked. I left sins unchecked for decades.

They kept me from experiencing intimacy with Christ. Now that I have experienced intimacy with the Father, Son, and Holy Spirit, I realize that what I thought was "no big deal" was actually allowing the bad father to impact my life more than my Good Father. I recognized that I never walked away from the sin nature that I was born with. I never chose to walk as a New Creation. I realized that essentially, I was "serving two masters," and since God demands, "…thou shalt have no other Gods before me" (Exodus 20:3), I was not even giving myself the chance to be intimate with God. Without intimacy with God, there is no Immeasurably More. Immeasurably More is not just blessing and favor. Much of Immeasurably More can be identified as freedom, power, and confidence. Although I had been saved of my sins, I was not free from them:

> For even though they knew God, they did not honor Him as God or give thanks, but they became futile in their speculations, and their foolish heart was darkened. Professing to be wise, they became fools, and exchanged the glory of the incorruptible God for an image in the form of corruptible man and the four-footed animals and crawling creatures. Therefore God gave them over in the lusts of their hearts to impurity, so that their bodies would be dishonored among them. For they exchanged the truth of God for a lie, and worshiped and served the creature rather than the Creator, who is blessed forever.
>
> Romans 1:21–25 (NASB)

Of all the sermons that I can remember around this passage, the above was always connected to the line that follows:

"For this reason God gave them over to degrading passions…" (Romans 1:26). The message was always focused on the sins of a whole spectrum of sexual perversion so prevalent today. Not until recently, after the renewing of my mind and the power of Holy Spirit working in me to give me the mind of Christ, did I realize that this passage should have been convicting me all of the years of my "walk with the Lord"—Christian-ese for my spiritual journey:

> …they…being filled with all unrighteousness, wickedness, greed, evil; full of envy, murder, strife, deceit, malice; they are gossips, slanderers, haters of God, insolent, arrogant, boastful, inventors of evil, disobedient to parents, without understanding, untrustworthy, unloving, unmerciful; and although they know the ordinance of God, that those who practice such things are worthy of death, they not only do the same but also give hearty approval to those who practice them.
>
> Therefore you have no excuse, everyone of you who passes judgment, for in that which you judge another, you condemn yourself; for you who judge practice the same things. And we know that the judgment of God rightly falls upon those who practice such things.
>
> Romans 1:29–32

If you just skimmed over that because you have heard at least two sermons from this passage a year for the past ten-plus years, then please bear with me as I break this down. Reading this passage with a "new mind" and with my spiritual eyes opened floored me. I found myself in the passage, which I had only applied to others before. This isn't just about "those sinners" who live a lifestyle that displeases God. We are those sinners that are living a lifestyle of displeasing God. We are separated from intimacy with God because of an unrepentant heart and unchecked sin. We are not experiencing More because we have exchanged the More that God has in store for us for the Less of living just as we always have. Bear with me as I go back through this passage with a nit comb. "For even though they knew God, they did not honor Him as God or give thanks" (Romans 1:21).

I know God. I have known Him my whole life. I was raised in a Christian home and went to a Christian elementary school. I may have been grateful, but I did not honor God. The "they" is me. How can you honor Someone when you don't respect them, do not revere them, or love other people and things more? How is letting pride, jealousy, selfishness, envy, and gossip pervade my life honoring God in any way?

"…but they became futile in their speculations, and their foolish heart was darkened" (Romans 1:21). Without a holy awe or proper fear of God, one can never expect to "know Him and the power of His resurrection" experientially (Philippians 3:10). We can know it intellectually, but experience is where you "level up." Head knowledge without experiential intimacy with Holy Spirit will be futile speculation of what Holy Spirit is truly capable of doing in our lives. Without seeking to live a holy life through the transformation of Holy Spirit, our hearts will remain dark with sin. Confession without repentance means that the darkness will return. The light will fade. The show will go on as it always was unfolding:

> Professing to be wise, they became fools, and exchanged the glory of the incorruptible God for an image in

> the form of corruptible man and the four-footed animals and crawling creatures.
>
> Romans 1:22–23

Knowledge of Scripture and ability to quote it is great, useful, and can bring transformation. God's wisdom, though, is a deep well going beyond this knowledge. Following the world's wisdom and remaining in the box that we were developed in is foolish. How can we embrace More if we don't seek out the wisdom of God? I exchanged the glory of an incorruptible, holy, and perfect God for prideful striving for importance, recognition, and notoriety:

> Therefore God gave them over in the lusts of their hearts to impurity, so that their bodies would be dishonored among them. For they exchanged the truth of God for a lie, and worshiped and served the creature rather than the Creator, who is blessed forever.
>
> Romans 1:24–25

Idol worship. I was my own idol sometimes. Sometimes, it was a celebrity, ball team, or Christian band. God basically said, "Okay, have it your way," and allowed me to follow the "lusts of my heart": obsessions with people, things, hobbies, food, and various forms of spending:

> …they… being filled with all unrighteousness, wickedness, greed, evil; full of envy, murder, strife, deceit, malice; they are gossips, slanderers, haters of God, insolent, arrogant, boastful, inventors of evil, disobedient to parents, without understanding, untrustworthy,

But Wait, There's More   73

unloving, unmerciful; and although they know the ordinance of God, that those who practice such things are worthy of death, they not only do the same, but also give hearty approval to those who practice them.

Romans 1:29

I have absolutely no idea how many times I have read the above verses and thought to myself, *Oh, those poor unbelievers, caught up in all of those sins that are keeping them from eternity.* Then I realized that half of the list above describes me.

Unrighteous—I have broken the Ten Commandments.

Greedy—I selfishly wanted control.

Full of envy—I often wanted what others have: experience or their relationships.

Deceitful—half-truths and omissions are still lies.

Gossip—I have disguised gossip as prayer requests.

Insolent—I show disrespect to God when I live carelessly and recklessly.

Arrogant—I recognize that the thought "*At least I don't sin like them*" is sin itself.

Boastful—it takes practice, but there is a false humility that is low-key bragging.

Disobedient—delayed obedience is disobedience.

Unloving—I definitely have not loved all my "neighbors" as myself.

Unmerciful—before Holy Spirit's renewing of my mind, I was happy when others got "what they deserved."

"Those who practice such things are worthy of death." I am worthy of death. You are worthy of death. Gossip? Yes, worthy of death. Arrogant? Yes, worthy of death. Deceitful? Yes, worthy of death. Disobedient? Yes, worthy of death. We are unclean before a Holy God. "The wages of sin is death…" (Romans 6:23a).

BUT WAIT, THERE'S MORE

"…but the gift of God is eternal life through Jesus Christ our Lord" (Romans 6:23b).

God is so gracious and kind. He has given us forgiveness for these, but I spent so many years forgiven and continuing to walk in these. I was breaking His heart and missing out on the Immeasurably More He had in store for me. In His power and strength, we can walk away from these and all of the other "sins that so easily beset us," as they are described in Hebrews 12:1, and embrace the More that God has in store for us. The exchange of Less for More can only come in the total surrender to God and acknowledging Holy Spirit's work in your life. More will only come when you turn your back on the Less that the bad father wants you stuck in.

Turn your back on the Less and seek first the Kingdom of God and His righteousness, and all these things shall be added to you (Matthew 6:33). "All these things" are "immeasurably more than all you can ask or imagine" (Ephesians 3:20).

Let's talk about how we seek first the Kingdom and righteousness so that we can step into More.

Chapter 11

The Kingdom cannot be contained. Righteousness cannot be found in the darkness of religion. For those reasons, and others we have yet to unpack, we have to break the fourth wall and smash the dim glass ceiling of our cube. Let the light inside.

When Holy Spirit first gave me the idea of this cube that either leads us to or away from our Lord Jesus Christ, I drew it on paper and labeled the sides. The more I looked at the drawing, I recognized how that "family wall," which I colored yellow to distinguish it from the others, represented my Grandma Bowden, who, even though she went to heaven when I was four, left a legacy of the importance of daily Bible Study. I recognized that the Thomas family Christmas traditions shaped my love for the Christmas story and the earthly origin story of my Savior. I remembered being connected to my best friend through her baptism experience. I did not even attend her baptism, but I remember that her braided hair was wet when I saw her that afternoon as she told me about her experience.

Once I determined that this cube of spiritual development was a logical concept, I went to Hobby Lobby and bought a clear baseball display case—a perfect clear cube four inches wide on each side. Holding it in my hand, I placed a clear label on each of its six sides: God's Word, family, relationships, culture, education, and eternity. I thought about how our actual individual walls are invisible but just as real as the six walls of the plastic box in my hand. I thought about how my church culture had taught me about gender roles and how my particular private Christian school education sheltered me from a great deal of profanity and rebellious friends, although I was still exposed somewhat. I thought about the relationships in my life, past and present, impacting me with subtle influences and shared experiences.

Relationships with people in close physical proximity allow us to break the fourth wall with people all the time. Eye contact, handshakes, and hugs are essential elements to any relationship, whether you meet someone for a moment or they are a life-long friend. Up until a couple decades ago, you could barely say that you had a relationship with anyone unless this proverbial fourth wall was literally broken. Sure, there are stories of pen pals and lovers separated by oceans, but the relationship changes when the first eye contact, handshake, or hug is given. Even today, we have video chats and can virtually make eye contact with many people that we have never been in an actual room with, but it is not the same as actual eye contact, a real handshake, or a bear hug.

God made us this way. God designed us to live in community. His trinitarian nature represents community, and as He made us in His image, He placed a need for us to be in community, to break the fourth wall with others, and to enter into relationships with them. He designed us to receive from and give to one another.

As you are formed spiritually, relationships are vital for you to encounter Jesus. He is placing people in your life to engage with, laugh with, learn with, share major and minor experiences with, and share everything that defines life. He is placing people in your life, whether literally or figuratively, who will point you to a relationship with Him. Despite the fact that the world we live in today offers every possible kind of virtual relationship, they are never fully satisfied. We were meant to intertwine our lives with others. Relationships bound by screens, photos, and/or video recordings limit the impact of those relationships. Our best, most treasured relationships are those where we are literally touched by others. Breaking whatever barrier is keeping you from contact, proximity, and a physical exchange is key to More. People enhance our lives and offer more ideas, experiences, and emotions beyond what we bring to the world alone. Jesus wants you to encounter others because "to love another person is to see the face of God" (Victor Hugo, *Les Miserables*). He doesn't want you to just encounter and break the fourth wall with people who introduce and point you to Jesus, but He is longing for you to break the fourth wall in your personal relationship with the person of Jesus Christ and Holy Spirit. Jesus Christ is calling you to break the fourth wall and seek out intimacy with Him.

As with any cube, if you remain in the cube, you will discover limitations. Jesus Christ is beckoning you to break the fourth wall, smash the glass ceiling, and discover more in your relationship with Him that will allow limitless freedom, blessing, joy, and peace. Break the wall, make eye contact, reach out, and touch Him. Right now. You do not need to be in a church, conference, or a Christian concert to do this. You can touch Him now. Call out to Him and ask Holy Spirit to meet you in this moment. Worship Him for Who He is. Worship Him through a song, read Psalm 51 aloud, pray out loud, and talk to Him as you would to a friend sitting in the same room, rather than someone on the other end of the phone at a Customer Service Center somewhere in India.

Does it bother you that He is invisible? Are you hesitant because He doesn't have skin on? How do you make eye contact with Someone you cannot see in the physical realm?

I sang songs in church my entire life that were prayers, asking my Savior if I could see Him. I never did. I knew I wouldn't in a literal way, so I assumed I was seeing Him. I wasn't. Why didn't I recognize Him, His power, the depth of His love, mercy, and grace? I was blind to those aspects of my Savior. Now, though, I do see Him! Still not with my physical eyes, but I notice Him working. God has opened my eyes to see the supernatural! God has given me a gift to see with spiritual eyes as if I am seeing with my physical ones.

It is supernatural. Hang with me. Don't close the book. You don't see Jesus, make eye contact with Him, or feel His embrace because you have recognized Him as Savior but not as Lord. You know a lot about the person that you asked to forgive your sins, but maybe you haven't turned and walked away from those sins. Perhaps you have even kept the unfathomable power of Holy Spirit housed within you in the proverbial box of an earthly family, education, culture, and relationships. Even though it has its foundation on the Word of God, it has been packaged up nicely and neatly in a box called religion.

It's time to check your heart. It's time to examine your relationship with Christ. It's worth a second look. Ask Him for More. He wants to give it to you. Stop seeking Jesus and open your eyes to see King Jesus. The same twelve letters in the same order, but take a step back, put a space between the E and the K, and see the King. King Jesus is more than your Savior. King Jesus is Lord of all in your life, or not at all. He is faithful to forgive us our sins and cleanse us of all unrighteousness (1 John 1:9). He is faithful and true to those words, but there's More. He wants you to know:

> For this reason, I bow my knees before the Father, from whom every family in heaven and on earth derives its name, that He would grant you, according to the riches of His glory, to be strengthened with power through His Spirit in the inner man, so that Christ may dwell in your hearts through faith; and that you, being rooted and grounded in love, may be able to comprehend with all the

saints what is the breadth and length and height and depth, and to know the love of Christ which surpasses knowledge, that you may be filled up to all the fullness of God.

Now to Him who is able to do far more abundantly beyond all that we ask or think, according to the power that works within us, to Him be the glory in the church and in Christ Jesus to all generations forever and ever. Amen.

Ephesians 3:14–21

As Paul prayed these words for the Ephesians, I am stopping right now to pray these words for every precious daughter and son of God that He leads to read them from this page:

> Lord, strengthen the one reading these words today, this moment, with Your power through Holy Spirit. May they feel You deep in their souls. Lord, may Christ dwell, abide, sit with them at the very core of who You have made them to be, and may they be in awe of You today. Give them faith beyond, deeper than they have ever known before. I pray that the foundation and family that you have planted them in represents love. Lord, may they see the roots and foundation of the love You have placed in their life. Open their eyes, Lord, to see Jesus as King of their life. Allow them to comprehend Holy Spirit. Your love for them is so deep, wide, high, and long. Allow your beloved ones

to have a fresh revelation of knowing You and the power of your resurrection. Fill them up, Lord, with You and Your Spirit. Fill them to overflowing today, Lord, right now in this moment. Give strength, grace, and unquenchable desire to break through any walls of pride that may be keeping us from fullness in You, from intimacy with You.

Lord, You are able. Lord, You are able to do all things. Lord, You are able to do Immeasurably More than all we can imagine. Lord, be glorified today and use them to bring glory to You through Your church, through Christ Jesus forever. Amen

I have found freedom in and through these words. My freedom, though, is not based on what I have done, learned, experienced, prayed, or testified to others. My freedom comes from laying down pride and idolatry in my life every single day and placing Jesus on the rightful throne of my heart, trusting in Him to direct my path, and denying my own understanding. (Proverbs 3:5–6)

Chapter 12

Breaking the fourth wall, seeing Jesus as King, and seeking intimacy with Holy Spirit makes the glass ceiling much easier to smash. In observing others, some people break the fourth wall but stay in their box. They find intimacy with Holy Spirit, but they are not perceiving life in light of eternity. There is a cap on their More because although they have found a true relationship with Christ, they are still performing on the stage that was created for them by their bad father. Scripture says that we are a new creation in Christ, but you must choose to step out of the old life, the old "man," and receive new sight, a renewed mind, a tender, humble heart, and new hands for serving others, and new ears to hear His voice. Intimacy with Christ is the same as intimacy in any other relationship: that it is unique for each individual relationship. Like your fingerprint, it will be unique. Your relationship should be a walk, a journey. You will have to step off of the stage and out of the cube in your own way and in your own time. The steps you follow, the choices you make, and the tangles that try to trap you in the old life will not look the same as those of your friend, pastor, mentor, sister, or cousin. Holy Spirit will meet you daily, hourly, or more often, right where you are and walk you into the true newness of life that the church talks about when we are baptized.

So, the following may not be the first step that you take into freedom, but it will be a pivotal one. Embracing eternity as the lens through which you view your mortality will allow you to see the Kingdom of God here on Earth all around you. This is not the only step or level of understanding that God is calling you to see. He is allowing you to learn more of Him and unlearn the lies that were set up for you in your cube. Ideally, once you embrace eternity and smash the dim glass ceiling above you, the other three walls will fall or will be easily pushed over, and you will find yourself "…like a tree firmly planted by streams of living water, which yields its fruit in its season and its leaf does not wither; and in whatever he does, he prospers" (Psalm 1:3).

Our perspective of eternity is dependent on three things: 1) belief, or not, in a literal place called heaven, 2) belief, or not, in a literal place called hell, and 3) the greatest amount of calculable time that we can wrap our mind around. Other contributing factors to our perspective of eternity are whether or not we: 4) believe in angels, 5) believe in Satan, and/or 6) believe in demons. Another possible factor to consider is whether the above are all abstract beliefs or whether you have a strong belief that any or all of the above impact the here and now.

Scripture gives evidence of all of the above. Scripture talks about an actual place called heaven where our trinitarian God resides and is accompanied by angels and all of those who were redeemed by Him before their deaths. Scripture talks about Satan and his fallen angels and how they are wreaking havoc on the Earth. Scripture also says that God decided that a man's life would be limited to 120 years (Genesis 6:3), and a lot of Americans got stuck on that statement and decided our focus should be limited to that. All the faithful churchgoers likely know the line from the poem by Missionary Thomas Studd: "Only one life, 'twill soon be past, Only what's done for Christ will last." So, we are all focusing on doing things in this life that will impact eternity, but we are not considering the fact that eternity is now, and we need not be bound in our thoughts by eighty or ninety years.

The other perspective of heaven that keeps us trapped and limited is how heaven is described as having streets of gold, pearly gates, no sickness, no need for a sun, mansions, and where the lion lays down with the lamb. We have been trapped by these words. Trapped by their literal definitions without taking into consideration what context we will find this perfection in. "Streets of gold" sounds great. Surely it will be beautiful. What if it is slippery? Will it be bricks of gold like in *The Wizard of Oz* or smooth like when asphalt is first poured? If there is a gate that is made out of a giant single pearl, where is the scallop that it came out of, or did God just speak it into existence? Yay for no disease. We won't need hospitals, medicine, or vitamins. Half of the drama in our lives will be taken care of, so what will we be doing? Singing? Floating on clouds? Walking around on the streets of gold chatting with people that we knew in elementary school but never found on Facebook? I hope you see the progression here. Heaven sounds nice but boring. Why look forward to eternity when it doesn't really sound that interesting? What is there to get excited about? Heaven on Earth. Heaven is now. Eternity for the unbeliever begins when death completely consumes them. Eternity for the believer begins when you are transformed, discover intimacy with Holy Spirit, and see life with eyes that see supernaturally beyond what is right in front of you.

Heaven on Earth can be realized when we fully commit to embracing the truth of Matthew 6:33. The journey to heaven on Earth from your current reality of Earth requires careful examination that leads to a beautiful exchange of our best life for His warm embrace of provision, blessing, and Immeasurably More than what we can ask, or imagine. This Scripture says, "Seek first the kingdom of God and His righteousness, and all these things shall be added unto You." You can't seek something that you don't know exists. Well, I guess you can. Many people search for wholeness in life, not knowing that it is only found in Jesus Christ. We hear stories of people searching for treasure but not knowing specifically what it is or its actual value. People search for their soulmate without knowing the actual person they are looking for in the world. I realized not too long ago that I was seeking the Kingdom of God, and I had no idea that the More I was looking for was wrapped up in the Kingdom of God. The Kingdom of God is a literal, yet invisible, legitimate governing entity that Jesus preached on many times in Scripture but that I, having been raised in church, never once had explained to me until two years ago. Embracing eternity means seeking The Kingdom of God and exchanging the following:

EXCHANGE	FOR
Achievements, Notoriety	Less
Riches	Wealth
The Seen	The Unseen
Lies	Truth
Self-Made Power	Supernatural Power
Fake Jesus	Authentic Jesus
Limited God	Unlimited God
Impotence	Power
Relative Truth	Grace and Truth
The Unseen	Vision
The Natural	The Supernatural
The Fake Supernatural	Unimaginable
Less	More
Now	Eternity
Tainted	Pure
Dark	Light
First	Last
Duty	Devotion

The left column is many of the mindsets and "lenses" of what tools, weapons, and resources we engage to "get through the day," "play the hand we were dealt," and make a feeble attempt at "seizing the day." God wants us to renew our minds and be transformed into a lens of More. A lens of More will exchange more tangible, corruptible, and concrete trappings of this world for less stuff and more Jesus. Consider the column on the right. Our cube has shaped us into believing that the supernatural, unlimited resources and Immeasurably More are not realized until we die and enter eternity. That's a lie. If you have confessed Jesus Christ, not only as Savior, but also as Lord of your life, and you have repented and walked away from the entanglements trying to trap you on the stage of the bad father, your eternity has begun; it is here now. You have unlimited power within you through Holy Spirit. You have unlimited resources a prayer away. You have access to supernatural wisdom and knowledge that will equip you to handle any scenario that the father of death, lies, and destruction wants to lay in your path.

EXCHANGE LESS	FOR MORE
Lies	Mindset
Entanglements	On
Selfishness	Righteousness and
Simple Sins	Eternity

The less you are living in is comprised of:

lies—told to you

entanglements—tripping you up from living rightly

selfishness—putting your desires before Christ

simple sins—the ones no one talks about in church

Sure, there are many, many, many people living in the less of drug addiction, porn addiction, other sexual immorality, theft, abuse of others, etc., but those are obvious, and many of those people are out of the reach of the church. But we, within the body of Christ, could reach them if we would repent of our Less, be truly transformed by Holy Spirit, and be emboldened by Him to reach out to those without the hope of Jesus all around us.

The bad father is known as the father of lies. You have been lied to your entire life about some things and have been given the truth about other things. The lies that you do not realize are lies that become "your truth" and are opposed to the truth found in Jesus Christ. You don't know what you don't know, so if you don't know that what you are believing is a lie, then you will not live out God's best for your life in that area. Our human nature does not have a proclivity to recognize truth without seeking it. Most of us don't seek it but rely on the cube we were raised in to determine truth from lies. Sadly, if you have not given over the direction of your life to the Good, Good Father, then you are being deceived and do not know it.

Omissions are just as bad as lies. Leaving out the truth is deception. My church culture omitted many parts of Scripture that shaped my understanding of truth. Although I relied on Scripture to be my source of truth, I did not have the whole picture because certain portions of Scripture were omitted or under-emphasized throughout my lifetime. This still happens weekly.

We need to take time in our journey to realize and/or recognize what parts of our cube are still impacting us. Do we need to unlearn false teaching? Do we need to seek out the truths that were omitted from our education on spiritual matters? Do we need to walk away from religion and embrace a Kingdom life? In the following chapters, we will identify the difference between religion and Kingdom mindsets. We will identify where we have embraced formulaic faith. We will learn how to seek Him and His righteousness first through a one-of-a-kind recipe for More in your life. You will have to put in the time and effort to seek Him for More and write your own recipe for spiritual success.

Chapter 13

There's more that we can exchange. If the abstract ideas in the previous chapter do not get you excited about the More in Jesus, then consider the other things that you can trade up. In church, we may sing about trading our sickness, shame, and pain. Have you ever wondered what you can trade up for in Jesus? Can we trade cowardice? Can we trade embarrassment? Can we trade doubt? Can we trade fear? Can we trade excuses? If the joy of the Lord is our strength (Nehemiah 8:10), and His strength is perfect (Philippians 4:13), then let's seek intimacy with Holy Spirit so that we can know, understand, and walk in a victorious Christian life. We begin by starting with small bite size pieces that, when we put them together, become a puzzle revealing a picture of Christ in us, the hope of glory (Colossians 1:27). What happens, though, when the sickness that you want to trade in for healing has you doubled over on the bathroom floor in such intense pain that you can't move and are a prisoner to the pain. We have to trust. We have to worship. We have to cry out to Jesus. We have to recognize that Jesus is using circumstances like this to draw us to Him. What happens when we sing songs about victory as believers of Jesus in church, and then we walk out of church, and our mind is filled with the voice of the bad father reminding us of the mistakes we have made sexually, financially, or for our physical health?

The above is an example of a religious mindset, of a life of living in Less and/or formulaic faith. Those of us having grown up in church often sing the songs, put on a happy face on Sundays, and hang on to the promises of God, relying on the stories of what He did in the past and/or what He has done for others, but do not experience literal trading of sorrow for joy, trading shame for confidence, or trading pain for healing. There is no true freedom in religion. Although there are many ways to describe religion, it is always found most easily in a home, relationship, or church that does not acknowledge the supernatural work of Holy Spirit in the here and now but leans on past workings and moves of God to fuel their spiritual fervor.

Jesus said, "Repent for the kingdom of heaven is at hand" (Matthew 3:2). The Kingdom is here and now, and those who practice repentance, not just repeating a prayer of confession but actively walking away from the pride and idols in their life, will experience and recognize the Kingdom of God on Earth. If the Kingdom is found in our trinitarian God, and He gave us Holy Spirit to live inside of us, then the Kingdom can be found within us in that intimacy with Holy Spirit. Salvation is everything, but He is more than everything. He wants us to grow, mature, and rise up into More.

If you grew up in a church culture similar to mine, then you may be unnervingly aware of not only how often I have mentioned Holy Spirit but also that I have dropped the article "the" from His name. So, let's talk about Holy Spirit. Many churches today are not talking about Holy Spirit. Some outright ignore Him. If mentioned in a sermon, the terminology used to describe Him lacks the power, amazement, and wonder that surrounds Him in Scripture. He is a mystery but not one to be ignored. He delights in our asking questions of Him, seeking to know Him more, and singing about Him. Why would we/should we ignore the power that is at work within us? Religion keeps Holy Spirit small in our mind's eye and in our understanding because a religious atmosphere, spirit, or culture is baked in pride and idolatry of self and tradition over the lordship of Jesus Christ and a fear and holy awe of God.

We will talk more about Holy Spirit, but let's stop for a

minute to say that any one of us can be said to be in the dark and be at the mercy of "not knowing what we don't know." Many Christians and the churches they attend are stuck in traditions and a formulaic faith that grows but lacks abundant growth or thriving. Many churches have constructed their own six-walled cube—just as influenced by the same six factors and just as binding as the cube of an individual. In your church, I pray the foundation is the Word of God, the Holy Scriptures. Does your church limit their understanding of the Word of God to the graphite on the page composed of the Old and New Testament, or do they acknowledge that the Person of Jesus Christ is also the Word of God, and He did and said many things that were not contained on the pages of Scripture? Does your church only accept certain translations of Scripture? Do they disregard translations that do not line up with their finite understanding of God the Father, Jesus Christ, and Holy Spirit? You may be a part of a religion rather than the Kingdom if any of these are the case.

Consider how the culture has impacted the framework of your church. This may be self-explanatory, but allow me to point out the fact that church in Charlotte, North Carolina, may resemble what is taking place in Portland, Oregon, but may not resemble at all what is taking place in Jakarta, Indonesia, much less in small rural villages of inland China. Of the half a dozen or so churches that I have been a part of in my lifetime, all have had similar schedules and programming that consist of weekly service with music, preaching, and opportunities for giving. All have had smaller life groups or Sunday school classes to facilitate discipleship. All have had special events to invite the "lost" to or provide opportunities for intentional evangelism. However, I realized recently that none of the activities and scheduled programming are outlined and are only loosely described in Scripture. Churches that boast of the effectiveness of programs, classes, schedules, and outreach activities are often trapped in a spirit of religion. Tradition and controlled experiences are elevated above seeking the presence of God. The presence of God is with us whenever two or three are gathered in His name (Matthew 18:20), but He wants us to experience His manifest presence—individually and/or corporately. Religious services do not create an atmosphere where Holy Spirit is invited to manifest His presence among His people. Religious services are often more for entertainment than true worship. If you do not believe that Holy Spirit manifests His presence in this day and age, ask Him if He does. If you are not accustomed to hearing Holy Spirit answer your questions, then start by asking Him to speak to you in a way that is unmistakable.

Education impacts every church in varying ways. Education, in lack or abundance, impacts the preaching, leadership, and quality of programming. Education may even impact the culture of a congregation. My husband and I once visited a church where it seemed like you had to have at least a bachelor's degree to understand the language used in the message. Do you know any churches where the Pastor does not have a Bible college or seminary degree? The lack of education impacts the church culture. I am not saying that God requires a certain kind or amount of schooling to equip anyone for preaching, but education does impact the culture of a church. The number of degrees that a pastor or elder has actually may impact the church more negatively than positively. Knowledge is not required for salvation, repentance, transformation, or a renewed mind. The fear of the Lord is the greatest indicator of whether or not the presence of God will be felt/experienced within a church. Proverbs says that the fear of the Lord is the beginning of wisdom. Wisdom is different from knowledge. Wisdom gives greater ability to discern. Knowledge puffs up, and the more knowledge you have outside of wisdom, the more susceptible you are to pride. I know that I have been so, so guilty of this. Because I knew and could apply Scripture to social issues and dilemmas, I saw myself as better than those who were biblically illiterate. I was prideful, and pride in my knowledge of Scripture actually separated me from my Savior. The fear of the Lord will transform pride into humility. Praise God, I am now able to accept anyone for any discussion in love. Holy Spirit gives me the grace to listen and discern what they say through His truth rather than my own. If they ask my opinion, I will probably give them one founded on Scripture, but He has also taught me just to listen, hear them, and see them. That's what He would do for them, and that's what I should do for them.

Some churches today are also quite territorial in areas of education. In what seems to be an attempt at controlling what their congregants are exposed to, there is little diversity in opinions shared on any given topic. Control is also stereotypical of a spirit of religion. Certainly, the Pastors and leaders have a responsibility to filter what is being taught within the walls, but why not teach their congregants to discern and discover for themselves? Religious churches keep their congregants dependent on their teaching. Kingdom churches teach them how to be so intimate with Holy Spirit that He will give them the discernment to hear His voice and know when information is not biblical.

Some churches are impacted by a climate or atmosphere of family. Similarly to the individual's cube, it is rare, but not impossible, to find churches that have been shaped by a close-knit, long-lasting leadership team that may even include actual family members in various positions on that team. This is an atmosphere for those who fear the Lord and elevate Him above the church itself, for those who know how to host the presence of Holy Spirit, and for those who are diligently seeking the Lord for Him to lead and guide the growth of the church in a healthy way. These churches abound with fruit; they make an impact in the community where they are placed and around the world through mission endeavors, and they are willing to let God use their resources and people in other ministries and locations. The same type of leadership can stunt the growth of a church if it operates in the spirit of religion. Churches bound in a religious mindset seem to be continually striving to make things work and do not believe that God still works and moves supernaturally. When everyone in the leadership is so tightly connected and has been operating the same way for decades, they are prone to "cap" what God can do in and through them because they don't "think outside the box." God does not follow a recipe, but these churches often do. They rely on their own efforts for results. These churches are often inward-focused, and even though they send people and money abroad, their actions, plans, and programs reveal that they want to maintain control, order, predictability, and "transformation" on their own terms. There is greater emphasis on bringing the unsaved to the church rather than equipping believers to go out and reach the lost in the world.

Religion will not break the fourth wall. Religion does not truly know the authentic Jesus or intimacy with Holy Spirit. The religious have not embraced what Holy Spirit is doing now. They are stuck on getting filled up on Sunday and getting their new fig leaves to cover their sin until next Sunday because they are stuck in their Less and are not truly walking in new life as a new creation in Christ (2 Corinthians 5:17). The religious keep trying to fix the old man and walk around with the chains and shame of their broken marriage, sexual immorality, spending, or food addiction. The religious talk and sing about the goodness of God but have no idea of the greatness that He offers. Religion will not smash the glass ceiling. The religious are the ones who start planning what they are going to wear when the rapture of the church takes place because they are convinced that Jesus Christ is coming back for us tomorrow. The religious hear about wars and rumors of wars and start adding the unsaved to their dinner-time prayers, but they won't pick up the phone to call those unsaved loved ones to see how they can be the hands and feet of Christ to them today. The religious cannot wait to get to heaven and sing about their victory but do nothing to prepare themselves for the jobs He has for us when we set up His Kingdom on the New Earth or imagine what life will be like in the mysterious cube city of the New Jerusalem. The religious have their souls soothed as they sing songs as prayers for Jesus to return because life is so unbearable, but they never stop to ask for Him to "Move, Jesus, move in my heart today."

Check your heart. Consider your church. Do you have a formulaic faith? Do you describe your relationship with Christ just like everyone else does in your small group? Is your spirituality predictable? Do you attend two services a week, one small group, read a devotional in the morning, and pray at meals and occasionally in the car? Do you give a tithe and one faith promise gift? Do you build personal relationships with missionaries carrying the Gospel to the four corners of the Earth, or do you rely on your church to determine which missionaries are worthy of your investment? Do you leave all the studying, Greek and Hebrew, and Bible Conferences to the pastors and teachers? Are your conversations in the sanctuary on Sunday after the service about how Holy Spirit showed up or the next football game? Are you saddened when Holy Spirit is not mentioned in services for weeks on end? Does it bother you that the music in church feels more like a concert performance than a vehicle to usher in the presence of God? There's more to church. There's much More.

Are you willing to exchange your idea of The Way, The Truth, and The Life (mentioned in John 14:6) for His Way, His Truth, and His Life? You probably have yourself convinced that there is no variation in The Way, The Truth, and The Life.

After all, "the" indicates the singularity of these words. A few years ago, I discovered that I had, in my mind, created "My Way, My Truth, and My Life" and had mentally substituted or replaced them with The Way, The Truth, and The Life that is mentioned in John 14:6, The religious are the first ones to remind you that Jesus Christ is The Way, and He is, but they are appropriating the wrong definition of "Way." Jesus is the means by which we come to the Father, but He is not a singular path. He is the door but there are different ways to approach the door. I did not come to Jesus the same way or manner that my husband, daughter, or best friend did, but we are all trusting in Him as the way to forgiveness of our sins. The religious will remind you that Jesus is the Truth, and He is, but there is more to Him, more to be understood, known, and accepted beyond what is contained in the sixty-six books of the Bible. Jesus as Truth is a bottomless well that will never be completely uncovered, even in eternity. Holy Spirit does not reveal the same Truths about Himself to everyone equally or in the same order. He may never have shown you how He curates the smallest details of your most significant life moments as He has done so for me, and I have never known Him to restore my sight as others have. The Religious will insist that Jesus is The Life, but do they mean eternal life? He is absolutely, 100 percent the reason that I once was dead in my pride, selfishness, anger, fear, gluttony, and other trespasses and sins but now have the Hope of life after death. However, there is more to life, eternal life, than just living forever. What once seemed like living in black and white, now I feel like I am living a life with all of my senses awake and experiencing His glory, going glory to glory in the Immeasurably More that life has to offer in Jesus Christ.

When I walked around in black and white, I had no idea that there was an alternative. When I was one of the "religious right," my soul was soothed by the ritual and tradition of practicing my faith through following the formula I was raised on. I realize now that what I thought were supernatural experiences were actually natural consequences or fabricated feelings. I was truly moved by music, messages, and testimonies, but left unchanged. When you operate in the Kingdom and have truly been transformed by the power of Holy Spirit, His music, His message, and testimonies of His miraculous interventions leave you forever changed and aware of the eternal impact. They produce a desire to see others experience More, and there is no longer striving and straining to share the Hope within me. The Kingdom that Scripture speaks of is an overflow of the restoration that relationship with Holy Spirit, Jesus Christ, and God the Father establishes when you stand to walk in a new life.

The undertones of religion are control, uniformity, and predictability. The Kingdom is none of these. Although God is sovereignly in control, One in His triune nature and "the same yesterday, today, and forever," He offers freedom, creativity, and unimaginable outcomes when a Kingdom mindset is embraced. I have let go of the list of dos and don'ts and seek to please my Savior because He is more than wonderful. I am confident in my position as His daughter and heir to the throne. I no longer walk in the shame of immoral choices, gluttony, and pride, among other destructive labels. I have let go of a need to please my pastors, teachers, and church leaders and the expectations they place on their congregants. I no longer feel guilty when I do not measure up to the prescriptions outlined by those leaders. I seek only to please my Savior as His Word outlines. I know now that I need not strive for righteousness. I have already been made righteous through the blood of Jesus Christ, that which covers me. I no longer seek the approval of men. I am approved by God. He loves me lavishly, and that is evident by how and when He speaks to me as well as the Immeasurably More He allows me to experience. There are some things that you simply cannot see until your eyes are opened to the Less you are living in.

Chapter 14

The most amazing discovery of More is understanding that religion creates an either/or culture, but the Kingdom offers a both/and culture. As you examine and unpack the structure of religious organizations and churches, the framework will become evident, and limitations on acceptable people, behavior, and actions will surface. Religion draws lines that exclude. Religion keeps everyone that looks and thinks like them in their particular box, will not break the fourth wall to allow Holy Spirit in, and does not recognize how what we do today impacts eternity.

Religion divides believers because it excludes the counterpart to what you place importance on. One example is when the religious say that there is only one acceptable translation of Scripture, they erect a wall between themselves and any other believers who use other translations of Scripture. When I discovered that my God is a God of both/and rather than either/or, I had a radical shift in how I viewed the Kingdom of God and His "co-laborers." The either/or mindset of religion keeps many followers of Jesus bound, limited, and ineffective. An either/or mindset lays a foundation of pride in the life of a believer and, sadly, is promoted by many churches through snide remarks and insults of other churches that come across as jokes from the pulpit.

In the Kingdom of God, we can see that God meets us individually in ways that are just as unique to us as our fingerprints. We have to learn to see what God is doing beyond the specific experiences that we have had and those we have witnessed immediately around us. Recognizing the fact that God works beyond the scope of human understanding is the first step. Equally as important is accepting the fact that others will understand attributes, characteristics, nuances, and ways of God that you yourself cannot even comprehend. Pride keeps us believing that God could not possibly work beyond our scope of imagination and understanding.

At the twenty-year running annual Passion Conference of 2020, evangelist Christine Caine gave a powerful message about how God wants us to metaphorically "dig up wells" in the church that have been filled with dirt, debris, and junk, clean them out and allow Jesus to fill them with fresh, Living water. This was a metaphor for how she believed our God is working through believers on the Earth today. At the climax of her moving message, she challenged the college students attending the conference at the Mercedes Benz Arena in Atlanta, Georgia, by saying that God wants to use all the means and methods that He has given in times and ages past to bring Living Water of the Gospel to our world today. We find ourselves competing and comparing with other Believers rather than digging for fresh water. We have every spiritual blessing in Christ (Ephesians 1:3), not just the ones we pick and choose. The old paradigm, the religious mindset, is one of either/or. It is time for the Church to embrace the Kingdom and to walk in the mindset of both/and. As she was describing what divides us as a church, she posed a series of questions, representing the either/or of church culture. I quickly recognized how this mindset was clearly a part of my own spiritual development cube—a characteristic evident in my family, culture, and educational development. As I recognized this, I simultaneously committed to ending the either/or mindset and embracing a both/and mindset…clearly represented in the mind of Christ once you discover the More of intimacy with Him. Here is the list that Chris Caine gave.

Does God require/use:

Faith or works?	Both
Male or female?	Both
Spirit or truth?	Both
Young or old?	Both
Skill or zeal?	Both
Is blessing attractional or missional?	Both
Should we focus on Evangelism or social justice?	Both
Gifts of the Spirit or Fruit of the Spirit?	Both
Which is more important: grace or obedience?	Both
Preaching or teaching?	Both
House church or mega church?	Both
Theological or practical?	Both
Understanding with the heart or head?	Both
This Earth or the new Earth?	Both
Counseling or deliverance?	Both
Medicine or divine healing?	Both
Discipleship or outreach?	Both
Traditional church or contemporary?	Both
Liturgical or non-liturgical?	Both
Holiness or relevance?	Both
Prayer or action?	Both

Did this list confuse you? Did it anger you? Did it excite you? Do you have the capacity for a life of both/and in Christ? Do you have the bandwidth for what He is doing at large on the Earth and recognize that His Kingdom is coming but is also already here among and within us? Not until you break out of your cube will you be able to embrace the big picture of what God is doing in and among His people on Earth. He wants you to embrace this bigger picture. He wants you to be open to His moving in ways that do not fit in your personal cube. Greater things are coming, and much for the Kingdom will be done among us, in the here and now, if we engage with Him and set our eyes on eternity. Our limited scope of what He is doing may limit how He uses us. He won't force you to embrace liturgical worship, but are you willing to see Him in it? Are you willing to encounter Him in a mega church, or can you only find intimacy in a small group of believers? Don't put a cap on what God can do!

We need to discuss how our individual mindset limitations have become corporate ones. We need to see how, although God is limitless and boundless, He often limits His moving and working among us when we mentally or culturally place limits on Him.

"And He did not do many miracles there because of their unbelief" (Matthew 13:58).

Just as Jesus did not do miracles in person in his own hometown because those who knew so much about His upbringing and humanity doubted His divinity, He may not do many miracles among those who preach and pronounce that the miracles of the New Testament do not occur today. Denying His power, the same today as it was then, seems to be like saying, "God, I don't accept that you are more than my mind can comprehend." Do you hear the pride in that statement? I see it. I hear it. That described me for the majority of my life.

I was raised as a cessationist. Everyone in my family, community, Christian school, and church culture affirmed that the operation of gifts of tongues, signs, wonders, and the like ceased after the Apostolic Age of the church. I cannot believe I ever fell for that. There are a lot of things I was taught or that were omitted in my biblical education that appall me as I consider their impact on my spiritual development.

I take no pleasure in identifying these deficits. My heart is broken by the fact that so many people I attended and attend church with are stuck in the mindset that God must fit in the box that the cube of their spiritual development has constructed. He is so much more. If you ask Holy Spirit to open your eyes to the supernatural, He will. If you believe the supernatural is reserved for Marvel and Harry Potter movies, consider where the ideas for these "fantasy" stories come from. Our bad father has us convinced that we have to compartmentalize the secular and the spiritual, the natural and the supernatural. I have decided to add it and a few other concepts to my both/and mindset.

Does God work in:

The natural or the supernatural?	Both
His Way or through my way?	Both
In the fire/trials of life or through them?	Both
For our life on Earth or for the eternal?	Both

Does God Speak through:

Scripture or experiences?	Both
People or places?	Both
Word or music?	Both
My thoughts or their thoughts?	Both

Secular lyrics or spiritual lyrics?	Both
Secular movies or faith-based ones?	Both

Can I experience Holy Spirit's presence:

In church or my home?	Both
At a conference or in my car?	Both
In nature or at a theme park?	Both

I make this argument not to make light of tradition, ritual, and structure within the body of Christ but simply to implore you not to put limits on when, how, and where God can work, speak, or show up. I also don't use this mindset to justify using online church as a regular "assembling" of believers. I am not saying that embracing a both/and mindset is all-inclusive. There are places in Scripture that clearly outline the either/or of walking in the flesh or walking in the Spirit, the either/or of choosing life or death, the either/or of lawlessness or legalism, and possibly others. Embracing a both/and mindset is about tearing down walls that divide us and helping us to see More. We see more of God, His nature, and His acts on the Earth. We see more of each other and how He made us all unique in order to carry out His perfect will. We see more potential in the fallen world around us. We will see more blessings, the cup half full, and even a cup overflowing. He spoke to me in the phrase, "It takes all kinds to reach all kinds." I believe Holy Spirit placed this idea in my mind as it relates to people, experiences, styles of worship, presentation of messages, specific scripture verses, and every mode or method that God uses to tear down walls within our own hearts as well as walls that divide us as believers.

This mindset shift is truly beautiful. As we discuss the contrast between religion and Kingdom, the either/or mindset will label the religious and both/and will be associated with the

Kingdom. An either/or mindset gives distinctives within faith that, in reality, are borders and boundaries within a denomination or organization. These distinctions are possibly intended to distinguish a particular church from the world, but in actuality, simply distinguish any given church from the belief statement of another. This mindset kept me blind to the fact that there is something odd about singing "They will know we are Christians by our love" while rarely spending time with or serving alongside other Christians who don't talk or think like I do. Even after four decades of following Christ, I know few people personally who voluntarily serve alongside Christians of other traditions, practices, and denominations. They may work alongside them at a school or at a non-profit, but they do not choose to do so. This has begun to cause me much grief, and if me, then how much more does it grieve Holy Spirit? Our distinctions from the world are important and necessary, but working hard to distinguish ourselves from other believers seems antithetical to being a believer.

Chapter 15

Superheroes enamor and fascinate the believer and unbeliever alike. We all have a favorite and tend to identify with one or two specific characters more so than the Avengers, Justice League, or Ninja Turtles as a whole. I believe our souls are wired for fantasy and the supernatural because we are made in the image of a supernatural being. Culture, in the hands of the bad father, has hijacked the supernatural and displays it in books and film for the purpose of distracting us from the actual supernatural activity in the world around us and for conveying thoughts and ideas that perpetuate a humanistic mindset over a Scriptural one. Some argue that our enemy uses such distractions to desensitize us to the supernatural all around us. Others say the enemy cannot create anything unique but merely copies what already exists. That leads to the conclusion that if those who come up with these fairy tales are being influenced by the bad father, then the inspiration he is giving them already exists in some form in some realm, perhaps what we see displayed on the big and small screen and in books is reflective of what is happening in the spiritual realm. The converse is true in that authors and movie makers inspired by The Original, Creator God, Most High, will create that which resembles His Truth, such as the *Chronicles of Narnia* by Lewis, *Lord of the Rings* by Tolkien, and contemporary stories like *The Warrior Prince* by Shirer, and *Then There Were Dragons* by Dekker. Reality can be seen in fantasy if you unpack and dig for it.

So allow yourself to consider a bit of reverse engineering as I describe for you a few kinds of churches among us, especially in the Bible Belt of the United States through the metaphor of two of the most well-known superheroes. This metaphor came to me one Sunday as I was sitting in a church contemplating how and why some churches experience growth in steady, even strides and others experience exponential, even supernatural, growth. I wondered why some pastors and teachers facilitate healings and deliverance while others only see conversion. What characteristics of a church pave the way for both? Are some trustworthy while others are not? Are some churches "faking it"? Can the concept of the constraints of a cube in contrast to freedom without a cube be applied to churches as I have applied it to individuals? Humor me as I present to you:

The Batman Church vs. The Superman Church

The Bruce Wayne Church and The Clark Kent Church

Let's refresh our minds on who these characters are and their basic differences. Then, we will proceed with a discussion of how they characterize evangelical churches in the United States in 2024. Batman is our vigilante hero fighting crime in the darkest of dark. His strength, tools, and skill are of his own making. His origin story includes losing his parents at a young age in a horrific crime and dedicating his life to his own brand of justice. His alter ego is Bruce Wayne. In his hometown of Gotham City, Bruce Wayne is well-known for his wealth and innovation. He is known as somewhat of a celebrity and is more influential because of his wealth than any other contribution.

Superman is not of our world. Superman comes from the planet Kryptonite, but no one realizes that when he first appears. He rescues the stranded, those in perilous situations, and overtakes criminals in their heinous acts. He is recognized as other-worldly as he performs acts through supernatural abilities and strength. His origin story also includes losing his parents in a tragic way but then being adopted by earthly parents. His alter ego, Clark Kent, allows him to lead a more typical human life when he is not rescuing someone or saving the day. Clark Kent appears to be average and ordinary. Superman, under the Clark Kent persona, positions himself as a reporter so that he has access to the justice system workings, politics, and breaking news so that he might be privy to the information that will call him into action as his abilities are called upon.

Obvious similarities between Batman and Superman are:

1. Both are seeking justice.
2. Both are fighting evil.
3. Both stand strong for those who are weak in some way.
4. Both do that which most cannot do.
5. Both were impacted by the loss of their parents.
6. Both are taken advantage of by the community they are a part of.
7. Both have resources that most do not have.

Obvious differences between Batman and Superman are:

1. Batman is human. Superman is not.
2. Batman bruises, bleeds, and breaks. Superman does not (except for in the presence of Kryptonite).
3. Batman primarily shows up at night. Superman shows up anytime.
4. Batman has X-ray goggles. Superman has X-ray vision.
5. Batman has lots of gadgets. Superman needs no gadgets.
6. Batman has lots of vehicles. Superman needs no vehicles.
7. Batman (Bruce) is wealthy. Superman (Clark) is working class.

Now that we are all on the same page, let's talk about how these superheroes represent the church in America today. I have been a member or active participant of a Bruce Wayne Church, a Clark Kent Church, and a Batman Church. I am familiar with some Superman churches but have never been an active member of one. As I describe the following, I hope you will see that I use this example simply to bring awareness to the differences and that which divides the church as a whole. I believe that God would have His Bride be unified and of singular mission and vision so that we can usher in revival in the last days before His triumphant return. I love the church. I cannot imagine my life without it. I am heartbroken by the division within it. I bring attention to this because I am convicted of the pride, arrogance, idolatry, and jealousy that I once practiced in the church. This metaphor may be extreme, but we are divided as a Church, and we are losing the battle that we are meant to fight: not one of flesh and blood, but the one against the spiritual forces of wickedness in the heavenly realm (Ephesians 6:12). That verse sounds like a movie plotline to me.

Our Father wants us to walk in His supernatural strength, love, and abilities as the ideal Superman Church possesses. He wants us unified, but yet the division continues, the comparisons continue, and the pride is palpable. A complete stranger walked up to my daughters and me in McDonald's today. He asked them where they went to school. They were in uniforms, which may be why he asked. Then he asked us where we go to church. We told him. The church we attend is well-known in our city and neighboring cities. He mentioned an event our church is hosting this coming weekend and told us about the connection his church has to the Christian band that will be playing at the event. We exchanged small talk for a couple minutes, and then he said of the event, "That's good as long as we keep it in the Baptist family and are preaching the Word of God."

Wait, what? I am not sure which of the following he represents, but that kind of opinion is why believers are divided. To hold to the opinion that one denomination is more acceptable in the sight of God is prideful. No church denomination label or lack of one is assurance of a congregation that is pleasing to God. As a church or individual believer in Christ, which of the following are you? Are you relying on your own intellect, experience, and study to meet your needs and challenges? Are you utilizing and trusting in the supernatural power within you? Do you consider that power to be supernatural? Do you realize the superpowers you have access to? Here are a few ideas to consider:

The Superman Church: The Superman church knows its powers and knows that they are not of Earth. We came up with the NOTW bumper stickers for this reason. We have an array of "powers" through Holy Spirit that are unexplainable. We have the power to heal, deliver, and save in every sense of the word—in the physical and spiritual realm. We are confident in our abilities because we are hidden in Christ, and Christ is our life (Colossians 3:3–4). We lend aid to those "walking according to the patterns of this world," whether they have believed in the Lord Jesus Christ for salvation and repented of their sins or not. This body of believers displays wisdom, power, understanding, empathy, and extraordinary strength. They bear the fruit of the Spirit (Galatians 5:22–23). We are still susceptible to Kryptonite, though, because we reside in our natural bodies in a fallen world. Whatever form our Kryptonite comes in, it weakens, distracts, and interrupts Father God's plan.

The Superman Church embraces all of Scripture, even the parts we do not understand or cannot quite come to grips with. We admit when we do not know but will seek the Father's heart for understanding. We do not omit scripture that is relevant to what we desire to teach or impart in discipleship. We interpret Scripture from the bottom up rather than the top down and desire that it be applied as it was originally intended for the original audience it was written for rather than seeking to adapt Scripture to fit current culture. We believe the entirety of Scripture is relevant for today, that redemption can be found in every book, that Christ can be seen in every book, and that ultimately, the Bible is a love story from cover to cover. The God Who created us loves us enormously, equips us for the life He has designed for us, and gives us the superpowers we need to walk in and live a victorious life over sin and death.

The Clark Kent Church: These believers, bless their hearts, know they are not of this world but walk, talk, and look just like the world around them. They may seem a little awkward around Batman and Superman churchgoers because they aren't arrogant and don't have money or confidence in the power of Holy Spirit. The Clark Kent church works hard, but it may not be obvious that they are working for the Kingdom. In fact, they give no acknowledgment to the Kingdom on Earth but simply refer to the Kingdom as other-worldly. They have disguised superpowers in Holy Spirit, but they do not access them in public, but most often only in prayer. Clark Kent believers often have a great deal of wisdom and excellent discernment but are easily mistaken for "regular Joes."

The Batman Church: This church, regardless of their denomination, contains the most highly educated and highly trained staff. The degrees, honors, published works, and platitudes abound among the staff. They are also quite wealthy. They can bail out any missionary when they need an emergency plane ticket home from the mission field for specialized medical care. They will load up a tractor-trailer full of supplies to help relieve those impacted by natural disasters. These churches are very popular, well-attended, and have packed-out services, especially at Christmas and Easter. The Batman Church keeps track of who and how many they help. They may not publicize it on social media, but they make sure their congregants know who they have helped, how many were saved at VBS, and how many boxes were packed for Operation Christmas Child. Keeping track keeps morale high, reminds us of our mission, and keeps us inwardly focused on what we are doing for the Kingdom to come. The Batman Church has all the latest programs, technology to broadcast services, and programming to entertain—regardless of whether or not Holy Spirit is acknowledged.

The Batman church generally does not acknowledge Holy Spirit. They believe He exists. They believe He resides within them because Batman knows Jesus. They don't really need Holy Spirit. If they pray enough and spend enough, then they will draw people to Jesus without Holy Spirit. Or will they? Even Batman accepted help from Wonder Woman when Superman was impaled by Kryptonite while they had to fight the Doomsday Creature created by Lex Luthor.

The Bruce Wayne Church: The Bruce Wayne church is primarily a social club. They want to enjoy their carefully curated, inoffensive, and enjoyable Sunday service and not see anyone there again until next Sunday. They get dressed up in their finest and sip coffee in the lobby just long enough to be seen and exchange small talk with one or two others. They may be attending church simply out of habit or tradition. They give their tithe because they were taught that good Christians do. They may have a lot of knowledge or experience, especially in their work, politics, or hobby. They do not invest too much personally, though, because they have scars from previous battles and/or church hurt.

This metaphor can continue ad nauseam because these types of Christians and the churches they represent can mix and match and are impacted by the Enneagram types, education levels, and regions of the country they are in. We can even go so far as to identify the "Wonder Women" who are like Superman with an air of feminism, the "Lois Lane's" who don't realize that Clark Kent is actually Superman in disguise and has supernatural powers until she has been rescued from peril multiple times, or "Jimmy Olson" who never catches on. If we are going that far, then we might as well talk about the villains in and around our churches. Some of the villains are obvious, but others have alter egos, just like Batman and Superman, and can be found in church as well. Consider Lex Luthor, Jack Napier, and Selina Kyle.

Batman and Superman had a face-off because Lex Luthor pitted them against each other. Let's think about that for a minute. Who is Lex Luthor in this metaphor? Isn't it obvious? The villain of our church scenario is the father of lies, the enemy of our souls, and a bad father to those who know no other. He may manifest as Lex Luthor or any of the others. He may manifest as an evil genius, shrewd businessman or woman, or an other-worldly creature/monster. Our enemy will pit churches against each other because it slows them down, destroys bystanders in the process, and halts Kingdom growth. When will we stop to realize that we are all on the same team and that Batman has just as much power as Superman when he acknowledges Holy Spirit and activates that power?

The man at McDonald's today took me quite off guard. I think in the moment I agreed with him. I don't agree with what he was implying. I quickly told my girls that the preaching of the Word is the most important thing for any church to do, but that Baptists are far from being the only ones who do. In the man's manner and tone, which was so casual and friendly, was a message of arrogance. Never in my life would I have been so aware of this, though, had Holy Spirit and I not been journeying through the deconstruction of my faith. Never in my life have I been so aware of how good and evil, light and dark, are so entwined within church culture, as well as secular culture.

It seems silly to ask if you believe that the church is devoid of sin, corruption, and manipulation. There is evidence of it by the boatloads. There also, though, seems to be an atmosphere of perfection within churches. Asking people about their church seems to generate automatic responses of either how good the preaching is, how good the music is, how effective the programs are, or all three. Within the church, on any given Sunday or Wednesday, it is more of the same. Boasting, maybe? Is it all really that positive, or are we covering up the negative?

If you are still reading, either I have angered you, and you want more ammunition for the hateful reviews or social media slander, or you think I may have a message that will lead to repentance. Hang with me a little longer. It's time to talk about Bruno.

Chapter 16

The beloved Target store within my hometown, actually within sight of my home, is being partially deconstructed. Recently, a combination of severe weather and a water main break nearby caused the foundation beneath our Target to crack and shift. Within a couple of hours of this being discovered, the store was temporarily closed, and the community overreacted on social media. How would they get supplies for their children to make Valentine's cards? Within a couple of days, the cracks in the foundation and ground were growing. The store remained closed, and we all, some literally, watched as the situation grew increasingly worse; the ground shifted as if there had been a mini earthquake, and the stock room of our Target was sitting on the fault line. Two weeks after the initial closure, the crack was so large, and the ground so dramatically shifted that we learned the store would be closed for a minimum of months while a portion of the store was removed, deconstructed, and it can be rebuilt on a reinforced foundation.

As I climbed the hill behind my house and looked across the valley where Interstate 64 lies over to the hill that Target sits on, the gravity of the situation sank in. Before taking the time to examine the damage from a mile or so away, I knew it was serious, but something struck me about the fact of how well I could see what was going on from so far away. The following day, the news broke about the plans to rebuild. As I thought about all I had seen with my own eyes, from news reporters, and from social media, Holy Spirit spoke to my heart a message that has been brewing for some time. Not all deconstruction is bad. Just like flipping a house, rebuilding after a disaster can often come from a structure, framework, or even a foundation that has been laid previously.

The American Church seems to overemphasize those leaders within who walk away from their faith. We have our own brand of cancel culture. Deconstruction is currently a buzzword associated with those who publicly renounce their faith. This sounds like something that the enemy has probably put his stamp of approval on and designates some of his minions to stir up attention for these individuals. Silencing the written work, video messages, or music of those who claim to have walked away from a relationship with Jesus Christ does little more than bring greater division in the church. Perhaps we could talk about the fact that deconstruction is not all bad. In some cases, deconstruction becomes a lifeline, the saving grace, or the redemption road for someone to rebuild stronger and thrive.

Reports that have been given on our local Target store have yet to give any information about whether or not there was any prior indication that the back corner of our store would ever literally start sliding off of the hillside it sits on. Not until there were visible cracks and separation was it clear that deconstruction was/is necessary. Although, in this case, it was impossible to ignore, consider how this is a metaphor for spiritual development and journey with Christ. You may have heard it referred to as a crisis of belief. In the summer of 2022, I came to my own crisis of belief. I was mad at the denomination that I have spent my entire life a part of as I began to discover portions of Scripture that were never preached on, seemingly omitted. I began to ask lots and lots of questions. I have decided that if you build a building, toy, or piece of Ikea furniture and don't follow the instruction manual, then you may end up leaving out important pieces and expect them to stand or operate properly without them. My faith did not work to its greatest potential because I was missing the understanding of a few important pieces that had never been taught to me in church or even the Christian school I attended K-8th. In particular, I lacked a clear understanding of what Scripture taught about the role of women, workings of Holy Spirit, the practice of fasting, and the concept of the Kingdom of God.

I hesitate to list the specific omissions from Scripture because the problem does not lie within the specific topics that were omitted but with the fact that those who have gone before me did not find it fit to take a holistic approach to Scripture. We stand on the shoulders of giants as we carry on the traditions of faith. We rely on the teachings of imperfect people who left this Earth for eternity sometimes five years before our birth, sometimes fifty years, sometimes 500–1,000 years prior. Do we stop to consider what they got wrong or what they omitted? Do we stop to consider what social and environmental challenges they faced that honed their focus on a particular topic or area of learning? Scripture is inexhaustible, and yet we seem to find a particular niche, or perhaps a few niches, and stick to them. And yet, because Scripture is inexhaustible, we can never grasp it fully in its entirety. There is one omission that needs to be addressed, but it is not specific to any one denomination and is common in many.

Hopefully, by the time you are reading this, you can Google Target, Barboursville, WV, and find that the red letters that currently say "temporarily closed" will have changed to green ones that read "open." As they rebuild, not only will they have to shore up the foundation, possibly even reduce the overall footprint of the store, but they will certainly have to replace many things: concrete block, cement, rebar, studs, sheetrock, wiring, HVAC ductwork, and all of the essential elements of the building. When you buy a house, there is always a "final walk-through" to be sure everything is working properly and in order, and certainly, there is also a "final approval" given when an addition is built on or a remodel is done. What if you were the regional manager of our Target, walking through inspecting the work, flipped the light switch to the stock room, and nothing happened? You may ask for the contractor to check the breaker box or try another switch. What if you went to ask the contractor why the lights weren't coming on, and he informed you that there wasn't any electricity running to the section of the store that was rebuilt? No power. No illumination. The HVAC was installed, and ductwork was run, but there is no electricity hooked up to run the system.

No power. No illumination. In 2022, in the middle of my personal spiritual deconstruction and rebuild, I realized that the cube of my spiritual development had not had adequate spiritual electricity running through, and I needed to rebuild stronger with the power of Holy Spirit. As a part-time real estate agent, I have been in countless houses and homes. Many of the ones I have shown to clients are empty, and one of the most noticeable characteristics of empty houses is electrical outlets. Where are they? How many are there? Are they in the right places, especially in the kitchen and living room? In newer homes, there is an outlet every six feet. In newer homes, there is always an outlet where the refrigerator should go, in the most likely place for a microwave oven and for the washer and dryer. This is not the case in older homes. Homes, especially ones that were built a hundred-plus years ago, have far too few electrical outlets, and often, the ones they do have are in inconvenient locations. Could this be a metaphor for your life? It was for mine. Is Holy Spirit only accessible in certain "rooms" of your life? Is He hard to find when you need Him? Do you have spiritual electricity evident in your life?

We don't know what we don't know. In my spiritual development, Holy Spirit was often omitted or ignored in messages and conversations. He is the More. Without including Him in the life you are building, you will never see circumstances in the right light. Without a relationship with Holy Spirit, you will never experience the supernatural power needed to get through trials and tribulations. Without Holy Spirit, you will never know the More or figure out the everything you never knew you always wanted.

If you are going to deconstruct your faith, you have to build it back on the Word of God through revelation from Holy Spirit, or else you will desert. Getting it down to the studs is a must, but if the foundation is the Word, you need not change that; just build back His way on the frame You have. If your foundation is culture, family, or education, then the back will fall off, just like the Target in Barboursville. I have deconstructed my faith because there were pieces and steps missing, not because I had to throw it all out. I added to my faith; I did not desert it or throw it out. I am not mad at those who taught and shepherded me. I love them. I have great respect for their faithfulness, knowledge of Scripture, and devotion to God. I am just sad because they seem to be missing out on the More that I have found, most noticeably in the Person of Holy Spirit.

When I first realized what Scripture says about Holy Spirit and many Scriptures that are overlooked at the churches I have been a part of for so long, I wanted to leave. So, I told God, through Holy Spirit, how I felt and asked Him why. Why were the first forty years of my life in artificial light, or low light, on who Holy Spirit is and the More that can be found in Him? Why were stories of signs, wonders, and miracles dismissed? Why were other denominations spoken of as "less than"? Why is the validity of revival in other churches questioned by those within my church? My line of questioning continued. I sat in uncertainty about how to rebuild my faith. I never wanted to walk away from my relationship with Jesus. I had already begun to experience many, many things I never knew I always wanted. I wanted to walk away from my church, though. They, collectively, had let me down. The answers came, but not to the questions I asked. The rebuild was put on pause, but not for long. Holy Spirit began to reveal to me His plan for my rebuild. He gave me answers to the questions I did not know to ask but were the right ones to ask. Holy Spirit showed me to stay for my kids, stay for my friends, and simply keep showing up for Him. Disappointment and a religious atmosphere are selfish reasons to leave a body of believers.

My family, unless Holy Spirit instructs otherwise, will not be leaving the church that we have been a part of for nearly fifteen years anytime soon. I am deconstructing and reconstructing my faith but not deserting our church. We will stay because they are offering our daughters a firm foundation on the Word of God. He is showing us ways and opportunities to teach our daughters about Holy Spirit's power at work in us today through conversations and experiences at home, in the car, on vacation, and in lots of places. We are staying because we know there is no "perfect" church because everyone everywhere is imperfect. We are staying because we may be able to point others to the power and More that Holy Spirit offers through conversations in the sound booth, nursery, parking lot, and lobby. We are staying because He told me that it is not time to leave, and His timing is perfect. He told us He still wants us to serve there and is providing us with teachers and preachers beyond the four walls of our brick-and-mortar church to challenge us and lead us deeper into understanding the parts of Scripture that were omitted from our spiritual development cube.

Holy Spirit showed me that just as there are sins that so easily entangle us in a personal way, the same sins can entangle us corporately. Pride is the sin that divides denominations from working together. Arrogance is the sin that separates us from the believers who worship differently than we do. Jealousy is the sin that robs us of celebrating with those who experience revival when we are in the wilderness. Selfishness is the sin that keeps us from collaborating on outreach events. Gossip is the sin that disguises itself as prayer requests and fertilizes the other sins. I am sure others can be identified, but before we can expect power from Holy Spirit, before He will unify us, and before He pours out His Spirit among us, we have to recognize what is entangling us corporately.

Don't desert the church. Deconstruct your faith if you must. Seek to break the fourth wall and smash the glass ceiling above you. Embrace the intimate relationship with Holy Spirit that He longs to have with you. He longs to show you More. He longs to free you from the lies, entanglements, selfishness and simple sins that are keeping you from Him and everything you never knew you always wanted in Him. Repent of these things, then come back to church and serve Him. Serve Him, not your Pastor. Love Him by loving your brothers and sisters. Give generously because you are giving to Him. Seek Him. Stop relying on others to lead you to Him. Do the work yourself. Go deep. Dive in deep to the More He has for you. Deconstruction can strengthen the church if done on the foundation of The Owner's Manual, Holy Scripture. Desertion fuels the work of the enemy.

Chapter 17

Current drone pictures of our poor neighborhood Target building show an excavator sitting just beside the newly formed cliff where the road and hillside are collapsing. The excavator is reaching into the gaping crack of the building and seems to be separating what is still attached and removing what has broken off. These images show shelving within the building, still holding merchandise. This is a reminder of the surprise that this all was to the store employees and regular shoppers just two weeks ago when the slippage began. Not only was it a surprise, but the severity of the problem escalated very quickly. This will not be a carefully planned out remodel of the stock room. This currently is a rescue mission to salvage what can be from the store and not let what has been damaged and directly impacted prevent a rebuild. Construction, deconstruction, and reconstruction all include debris. Deconstruction usually requires demolition. Demolition removes the old, useless, or damaged, but sometimes, demolition can damage things that were still useful or could be repurposed.

What might be the debris of our spiritual deconstruction? If you realize that your faith needs to be deconstructed, that the sheetrock needs to be torn out of the walls of your spiritual house because it was never wired for the electricity of Holy Spirit, then there will be some debris you have to deal with. As you take your sledgehammer to the walls, you may discover some black mold, too. Recognize that seeking Holy Spirit for intimacy and More will reveal some figurative debris in your life, and possibly some black mold will need to be addressed. If you build back without addressing these two issues, you will likely find yourself deserting or living in Less again. The debris is the external habits, practices, idols, and traditions in your life that keep you from holiness. The black mold is the internal entanglements of sin that the enemy wants you to justify as being okay to hang on to.

Examining your cube may reveal a lot of teaching about the enemy of our souls, Satan. Some say we give him too much credit and that most of what keeps us trapped in tangles is ourselves and keeping ourselves as King or Queen of our life rather than Jesus. I agree. Others say we need to know more about him, how he works, and the powers of the darkness of this world that we are wrestling with. I agree. Some say ignore him, and I believe there are times that we should ignore him. James 4:7 says, "Resist him, and he will flee," and I have experienced that promise in a very literal way at times. Some say that second only to asking Holy Spirit to fill you when you get up in the morning should be declaring that the enemy has no hold or power on your life, and I can see a spiritual benefit, though I have never practiced that. I have read books about defeating the darkness, I have listened to podcasts, and I have sat through seminars about overcoming. I have decided that it does me no good to be ignorant of what the enemy is and is not capable of doing. I have also decided that focusing too much on his plans to steal, kill, and destroy me will distract me from walking victoriously through life. So, we are going to give him a bit of real estate in our discussion and the Less that he wants you to stay stuck in, but only a bit. Ask Holy Spirit to guide you into recognizing his tactics, and beyond that, your study of the bad, bad father is at your own discretion.

The Enemy

"A roaring lion seeking who he might devour" (1 Peter 5:8).

He tempts (1 Corinthians 7:5).

He deceives (2 Corinthians 11:3).

"He was a murderer from the beginning…" (John 8:44).

"He is a thief who has come to steal, kill, and destroy" (John 10:10).

You are familiar with the jerk-faced turd, I am sure. The problem does not lie in believing that he is who Scripture describes him to be but in being blind to the broad-brush approach of his tactics. The problem for most is not recognizing murder, theft, and drug addiction as wrong but recognizing that gossip, pride, and food addiction are equally as wrong. All sin unmakes us and separates us from intimacy with Father, Son, and Spirit. Our bad father wants us as far away from experiencing More in Christ as he can get us. Idolizing your children and putting them before God's plan for you will separate just as quickly as lying about where you were on Saturday night. Our bad father wants us to lose the ability to hear the voice of The Good Shepherd and will distract us with the static of news reports, social media posts, and texts from those who don't know Christ. Our enemy screams at us through tragedy, trials, and entertainment while the Bread of Life prepares a table for us to feast on His goodness, provision, and love. Who will you choose?

The same enemy who entangles us in distractions, lies, pride, jealousy, gossip, and the like uses distracted believers to bring the same sin into the church. These go unnoticed as we put on our smiles, sing real loud, and follow the prescribed routine of Sunday services. We bring the enemy with us on Sunday morning because we never told him to leave on Saturday night. We bring him with us in the sanctuary as we selfishly wonder why they sat in our seat, the same seat we have sat in for the past ten years. We humor him as we walk on by that aisle without speaking to the visitor sitting there. Our mind wanders to the celebration of sin we watched on the 75-inch screen at midnight, and we miss hearing Holy Spirit speak to us through the song lyrics. Some of us even take him on stage with us as our vocal performance drips with the invisible pride in our perfect pitch and how we have relished the compliments on our beautiful voice. He is there, knowing he could be dismissed at any moment by a simple word but expecting to be accepted by those checking their text messages as they navigate away from the Bible app on their iPad, or he is simply allowed to hover as we sit week after week without considering how long it has been since we felt the presence of the Lord among us during service.

Is Satan literally in the church service I attend on Sunday mornings? Probably not. He is by no means omnipresent. Is he visiting your church this week? Probably not, for the same reason. Is his spirit there? Absolutely. The lies, gossip, addictions, immorality, anger, pride, idolatry, and so much more are carried into church gatherings by anyone who calls Christ Savior, but has yet to call Him Lord.

We don't talk about… Lucifer. I do not think he deserves much real estate on a page or much air time from the pulpit, but I do wonder why we are not talking about how Holy Spirit can equip us to overcome his tactics, take back what he steals from us, revive what he kills in us, and rebuild what he destroys in us.

The Black Mold

If you want to discover More, you have to deal with the black mold. You may be like me, many believers are and grew up in a tradition of going to church, praying, and having a quiet time with Jesus or family devotional times. As I deconstructed the education, family, and culture walls of my cube, I discovered the black mold of sin that had to be dealt with before I could find true intimacy with Holy Spirit. I had to call it out and confess it before I could find complete freedom from the sins that so easily entangled me. Not only did I have to confess it, but I also had to ask Holy Spirit to show me how to rewire thought pathways in my mind and rewrite habits and traditions. This has been a process that I am still working through. I currently have never experienced such freedom from the sins that get me tangled up the fastest, but I have to be aware of the triggers and temptations specific to me so that I can call in backup from Holy Spirit to take thoughts captive, put down the spoon before I eat the whole pint or tell a half-truth to my kids.

If we are going to talk about sexual immorality, infidelity in marriage, murdering children in the womb, and drug addiction in church, why aren't we talking about the sin of pride, gossip, jealousy, and outbursts of anger? The church is supposed to be a hospital where people can heal from the damage of sin. Pretty much every church that I am familiar enough with to speak of or recommend to others is spending a lot of air time trying to help people heal from the "big stuff" like spiritual cancer, spiritual dementia, spiritual lung disease, and spiritual diabetes, but are leaving people to fend for themselves when they struggle with spiritual colds, flu, rashes, and allergies.

The Debris

How do we clean up the debris left from deconstruction? The debris from tearing down the walls, or maybe just pulling out a few bricks from the walls of your family, culture, and educational framework, is inevitable. It reminds me of trying to navigate through the stuffies, LEGOs, Barbies, plastic food, and dress-up clothes on the floor of our toy room. If your kids don't tidy the toy room after they play, then the next time you enter, it will be like going through a minefield. Be sure to put your shoes on; there may be some scattered LEGOs in there. They will be small enough to be overlooked but strong enough to bring you to tears. You may find that some relationships need to be downgraded. You may discover your spiritual mentor has become a spiritual peer. You may have to take another route to work because you are spending too much at your favorite coffee shop. You may have your kids ask why you don't buy the ice cream that tempts you anymore.

Holy Spirit will equip you with what you need. Draw near to God and He will draw near to you. Say, "Not today, Satan," when you go shopping and ask Holy Spirit to remind you what you need to buy and not be distracted by what you want to buy.

Just like the fact that the word "corporate" means a big group, a change in church culture, practices, and atmosphere is going to take a big change—many coming together as a result of experiencing personal revival. If we recognize the debris, we can ask Holy Spirit to help with the clean-up. It seems we have believed the lie that everything is black and white, either/or, but we need to take the time to examine the gray areas and not just lump everyone in the church into a labeled group. This manifestation of pride leads to the thinking, *At least I don't sin like they do*. These lesser-spoken sins, symbolized by the metaphor of black mold, give us a false sense of security and lead us to believe "we are right with God" because we don't "smoke, cuss, drink or run with those who do."

Living in the Less of lies, entanglements, self, and simple sins keeps you from intimacy with Holy Spirit and from God's best for your life. Living in Less is pretending that pride is not a sin, idolatry doesn't count when the subject is your kids, complaining goes unchecked, sugar and shopping aren't addictions, fear of anything is not a sin, and "I'm not lazy, I'm just trying to get through this." God opened my eyes to each one of these in my own life. It has taken years because He was so gracious to progressively reveal these things to me rather than strip them from me through some devastating loss, illness, or tragedy. If it were not for the grace of God, I would not have had my eyes opened to these things or learned to walk in freedom from them.

Perhaps the bad father is a curator in his own right. Our Good, Good Father is the curator of More in our lives, but the devil and his minions also know the effectiveness of distracting us with glitter and delicacies that keep the average Christ follower focused on the things of the here and now rather than the glory of that which we will spend eternity living in. #Iamblessed accompanies vacation photos, sweepstakes wins, "fortunate outcomes," answered prayers that were actually natural consequences, championship wins, and decisions that turn out for the best. Few require actual faith or intimacy with Holy Spirit for His perfect will to be revealed.

No, there are no perfect humans, churches, jobs, trips, schools, or holidays, but they can be More when God-Father, Son, and Spirit are given Their rightful place when believers see Him as He is, they repent of what is unmaking them and separating them from Him, and they seek to be Holy as He is Holy. I have been blessed by visiting dozens of different kinds of churches: Methodist, Catholic, Presbyterian, Anglican, Greek Orthodox, Episcopalian, Nazarene, Pentecostal, non-denominational/Bapti-costal, Church of Christ, Assembly of God, Four Square, and a bunch on the west coast and in other parts of the world that I cannot remember and the same is true for all of them: There are many religious people within them who have no real relationship with God, there are those within them who love the Lord with their mind, body and strength, most of them all have the same goal of seeing Jesus lifted high and people come to the saving knowledge of Jesus Christ. The greatest commonality among them, though, is a lack of the holy fear of God, a lack of preaching on true repentance, little to no preaching on the Kingdom of God, and few truly transformed souls. We, as the church, know how to get people to Jesus for salvation, but our discipleship methods are not transforming lives.

We cannot transform lives. We, in the church, can show our own how to clean up the debris of their former or current life, but only Holy Spirit can transform lives through true intimacy with Him. I cannot repent for you or you for me. Intimacy comes from true repentance, often a process that can take years. Holy Spirit takes us on a journey of refining. The closer we get to the refining fire that He is, the more the Less (lies, entanglements, selfishness, and simple sins) comes to the surface of our lives. When we repent and walk away from things like overspending, overeating, arrogant attitudes, and prideful posts, we go deeper with Holy Spirit. We transform our hearts, minds, and lives to the true image of Jesus. Only then can we authentically represent Him to the lost and dying all around us. The Less in our lives is like the ropes that bound Shadrach, Meshach, and Abednego in the Fiery Furnace. When they were in the fire with Jesus, those ropes burned away, but they were not hurt—they did not even smell like smoke when they walked out, but they were closer to Jesus. They had stood in His Presence while they were in the fire (Daniel 3).

I was raised to believe that the presence of God is not felt in tangible ways. I now know that is not true because I experience His presence regularly. I was raised to believe that the main goal of a believer is to save souls. I now know that God wants me, personally, to teach other believers about His Kingdom on Earth and His presence. I was raised to believe that a "sinner's prayer" had changed my life. I now know that the heart and message behind Psalm 51 is what an authentic sinner's prayer should sound like. I was raised to believe that what was taught in my church was without error and had a better message than other denominations. I now recognize how that belief cultivates pride.

The cube that was my own was full of debris and distractions from the truth. Once I started seeking Holy Spirit and the Kingdom, breaking the fourth wall and smashing the glass ceiling, I began to see the More. I see now truth that was omitted for four decades jumping off the pages of Scripture for me. I see Holy Spirit moving beyond just a few people walking the aisle on a given Sunday morning. I hear Holy Spirit's voice daily, giving me wisdom and discernment and teaching me just like Yoda taught Luke on the Dagobah System. I recognize how He is curating my life so I will experience More with Him in relationships, in gaining knowledge, in His creation, and in the experiences that are made by His design. The hot mess express of my life has become a beautiful blend of all things working out for my good because I truly, unequivocally love God and have been called according to His purpose (Romans 8:28). I have no regrets. Repentance has ripped my regrets to shreds, and I am now on a mission to take back what the bad father stole from me.

Chapter 18

One of the hardest parts of deconstructing your own spiritual development, relationship with Christ, and the religious traditions you have been raised in will be the tidal wave of anger, disappointment, and regret that is likely to wash over you. This may come all at once, as it did for me initially as I finished reading the final chapter of a particular book, or it may come slowly as a series of personal revelations come to mind. More than likely, it will be a combination of the two. This is the bad father's "last stand," his Alamo attempt. From my humble perspective, this is actually a crossroad moment for many people when they decide to stick with their faith and rebuild stronger or walk away. This same moment comes for many Christian marriages. There is a moment, I have a vivid memory of mine when I was fed up; the last straw had fallen to the ground in an argument with my husband, and I knew I was at the moment of deciding whether or not I was going to remain faithful to the promise that I had made to Him of "divorce is not an option." Those are just words the day you get married. There comes a time when those words become a literal choice. The weird part is that it rarely happens at the same time for both people in the relationship.

Your relationship with Jesus Christ is essentially a marriage, too. Deconstruction can lead to walking away from your faith, just like believers walk away from their marriages every day. The difference is that Christ is the perfect groom and has been every single day since you accepted Him as your Savior. He has been waiting for you to give all of yourself to Him and let go of the lies, entanglements, selfishness, and simple sins in your life. True transformation in your marriage comes with embracing Holy Spirit and repenting of all the things that are unmaking you. There is a crossroads moment of surrender. The bad father will distract you at the crossroads of continuing to walk in Less or in choosing More. Returning to the world will be deciding to walk in Less. Repenting from your former life will open the door to More. If you open the door to More, you welcome Holy Spirit to consume you, not just reside in your heart/soul. The enemy will bring sickness into your life, or you will receive word of the passing of a family member; you may find yourself suddenly without a job or maybe with a car that doesn't work. He is relentless. Crap happens in life when we are at that crossroads, and even if he didn't literally cause it (maybe he did), the enemy orchestrates distractions when we are standing at the crossroads of choosing Less or More. Sometimes, the distraction is a faux More… An opportunity that we need discernment from Holy Spirit to know who is sending it our way.

Choose More. Choosing More is walking away from lies when God has revealed His Truth to us. More means walking away from all of the sin that we have dismissed as "not that bad" our entire life. My addiction to sugar caused and causes me much inflammation in my joints and worsened my acid reflux to the point that I was spending thousands and thousands of dollars on medical tests and procedures with no income to pay for it. I wish I had sought Him sooner rather than take medical advice that was based on a checklist rather than my personal circumstances.

Repentance rips apart regret, but it may not completely remove regret from your mind. Repentance will definitely allow you to walk in More, and the regrets will diminish and possibly fade away. When I repented for my sin of not taking care of the "temple" that God had given me, abusing it, and letting bad habits unmake me physically, sugar lost its hold on me. It was a process at least seven years in the making, but I walk in freedom now. I remember that just a handful of years ago, I could not prepare any cookies, muffins, or cakes without sampling the dough, icing, batter, or finished product. It is strange to think back on it, but all of the willpower I could muster would not be enough. I would always swipe a lick. One lick led to five or six; sometimes a spoon would be pulled out from the drawer, and before I knew it, my stomach would start hurting because of the hundreds, maybe thousands of empty calories or the inflammatory sugar I consumed in a matter of minutes. I was blind to it as a teenager, young adult, and young mom, but once the arthritis and acid reflux began impacting my daily life, I asked Holy Spirit to show me how to connect the dots between it all. He did. Although I still carry some extra weight, I am losing some little by little, and in a year or two, with His help, I will return to a healthy weight for the first time since 2007.

Repentance dismantles the effectiveness of regret in your life. Regret feeds the shame cycle—that cycle of feeling guilt and shame and resolving to change and for a brief time feeling success but along the way becoming overwhelmed because you are trying to do a supernatural work in your own strength and having a breaking moment, splurge or binge that brings the guilt and shame back. Repentance will restore you to a right relationship with Holy Spirit, and He can and will equip and empower you to break the chains that are binding you. He broke a sugar addiction off of me, a spending addiction off of me, the idolatry of being a "collector" of Star Wars memorabilia, gossip, and pride. Although soft-spoken, the pride I felt in "living biblically" and considering myself better than those who are trapped in destructive lifestyles consumed me and impacted my choices of who and where I would serve Him for years and years. Praise God He was patient with me and allowed me to step into humility. Humility looks much better on me than pride:

> Therefore, as God's chosen people, holy

and dearly loved, clothe yourself with compassion, kindness, humility, gentleness and patience. Bear with each other and forgive one another if any of you has a grievance against someone. Forgive as the Lord forgave you. And over all these virtues put on love, which binds them all together in perfect unity. Let the peace of Christ rule in your hearts, since as members of one body you were called to peace. And be thankful.

Colossians 3:12–15 (NIV)

I read this for years and tried my best to be all those things: compassionate, kind, humble, gentle, patient, and forgiving. It was just like a shame cycle or a sin cycle. I did great for a while, but always failed trying to accomplish these on my own. I would even pray and ask God to help me with these, but I didn't realize that the Less I was living in kept me from accessing His full power, the power that comes from Holy Spirit within us. We cap the effectiveness of the power of Holy Spirit within us when we leave the sins of Less unchecked, simmering on the back burner of life.

Consequences Magnify Regret

I still have one major regret from my faith-filled life that was not totally transformed by Holy Spirit until 2017. It still "hangs over my head," so to speak, and it has not been resolved. I have broken the bondage of a sugar and spending addiction and walk in freedom most days; I have asked forgiveness for prideful advice I have given friends that was not beneficial, I have learned to resist the urge to disguise gossip as prayer requests, and I have learned how to diffuse my anger before I have an outburst, but the consequences of lacking the faith for God to provide for me financially still appear in my life, usually once a month when the bill comes from the company that holds my student loans and the local hospital.

In my teens and twenties, I remember singing a gospel song, "He's an on-time God, yes He is! He's an on-time God, yes He is! He may not come when you want Him, but He'll always be right on time! He's an on-time God, yes He is!" (Dottie Peoples). I believed with everything I could muster that His timing was perfect. I would have conversations about how He answered prayers at just the right time. He gave me answers for life choices at the perfect moment. However, now, in retrospect, I said something that I and my family did not walk out. Apparently, I believed that God showed up in the "11th hour," but did not believe that He was a God that would show up at 11:59:59. I have since learned that not only does He show up at 11:59:59 but that sometimes it is okay if He doesn't show up until 12:00:01.

The consequences I live in now because I believed my God was an eleventh-hour kind of God, but not an 11:59:59 God, are tens of thousands of dollars of student loan debt from twenty-five years ago. The God I knew then was Jehovah Jireh. He was my Provider, for sure. I did not know Jehovah Shalom, the God who is my Peace when the money is not there. This was several years before I was educated in how to biblically manage money, but even once I was, I always went to credit cards if my God didn't show up by the 11th hour, not realizing that, even for me, He could gloriously show up at 11:59:59. Plane tickets for mission trips, college tuition, and phone bills were charged because I did not have the knowledge or experience to know that Holy Spirit will not withhold from His children any good thing.

Twenty-six years after graduating college and twenty-three years after graduate school, I am still getting a monthly bill that reminds me that I believed God would provide but that I had to take measures into my own hands if His timing did not line up with mine. I regret this, and hindsight has been 20/20. I did not pass the tests He placed in front of me in 1995, 1996, and 2000, to name a few. Now, though my debt still lingers, I do not make that mistake anymore. If the money does not show up for a project or event, then He has something better waiting for me at 12:00:00 or 12:00:01, sometimes a different plan or path altogether. I spent so many years prideful in the idea that I knew better than God how my life should unfold. Mission trips are good, important, and impactful experiences. Surely, God wanted me to go to tell people about Jesus in Australia and Papua New Guinea. I will just charge a little bit, and He will provide me with the job to pay off the credit card bill when I return. What greater, deeper faith I would have walked in years earlier if I had taken the approach of if He doesn't provide for this voluntary trip, then maybe I am not supposed to be a part of it. My family, culture, and high school teachers led me to believe that I should go to college immediately after high school and that going into debt for a four-year university was far superior (can you hear the pride?) to continuing on at community college. Wow, how arrogant I was all the while convincing myself that that was God's best for my life.

If Only

The phrase "if only" may pop into your mind as you realize what the bad father has stolen from you. Perhaps, like I did, you will wonder why you couldn't have been experiencing years or decades of More that God had planned for you. Let Holy Spirit overwrite these thoughts. Romans 8:28 says, "And we know that God works all things together for the good, to those who are called according to His purpose." As you ask Him to be Lord in your life, and you trust the Lord with all your heart and lean not on your own understanding, acknowledge Him, and He will direct your path. (Proverbs 3:5–6). This verse still reads and means the same as it did when I was a senior in high school trying to figure out how to pay for a college education, but now so much more. The word "all" pierces my heart. I quoted the verse, but He did not have *all* of my heart, and there was Less in my life that separated me from intimacy with Him and kept me from hearing His voice clearly. I heard His voice clearly for the first time at the age of fourteen; I vividly remember being in my small, stuffed-animal-infested bedroom and hearing Holy Spirit tell me that He wanted me to be a missionary. The enemy twisted that unmistakable calling into the lie that I had to figure out myself how exactly to pay for the lifestyle of a missionary. Faithful is He Who calls you Who also will do this (1 Thessalonians 5:24). I now walk confidently in the knowledge that this is the whole truth, not a half-truth. My God shall supply all my need (but not always all my want) according to His riches in Christ Jesus (Philippians, 4:19). Trusting Him for financial peace requires deep intimacy, or at least strong resolve.

If only my parents, my teachers, my friends, pastors, other family, and adults in my life had known Holy Spirit like I do now as they were impacting my life. I did not make financial, personal, or educational decisions in a vacuum then, and I do not now. Transformation through repentance and giving Holy Spirit total lordship has allowed me to recognize how many who influenced my life did so in such a way that was a result of their own spiritual development, which turns out to be similar to mine. I was impacted by parents, family, friends, teachers, pastors, and others who did not have a holy fear of God so pure that they could show me how to give my heart fully in surrender to Him, trust Him fully, and not lean on our own understanding. They had the verbiage to talk about these things, but the More was missing, and we were all stuck in Less. Essentially, they taught me from an understanding that God was limited by time and space. They conveyed that He was a God who no longer performed signs, wonders, and miracles. They conveyed that grace saves us through faith but that we have to do our part for God to fulfill His calling in our lives, and sometimes our part is going into debt. This is a lie from the pit of hell, but one that the people who constructed my cube believed themselves and conveyed to me. They did the best they could with what they had been taught and what they had experienced. They taught what they knew and maybe never had checks show up in the mailbox the same day that rent was due when their bank account was empty. I believe it was the result of their prayers, lifting me up to the Father and interceding for Him to use me, lead me, and bless me, that I was able to meet Holy Spirit in His fullness in 2018.

I have so few regrets now, and the ones I have pale in contrast to the More that God allows me to walk in daily. You can watch your regrets shatter, diminish, and lose their power over you, just as I have. Your story will not look like mine. How could it? Your story of transformation and trading a life of Less for a life of More comes about through partnership with Holy Spirit and no one else. He will allow you to write your own recipe for intimacy, success, and more in Christ!

Chapter 19

"Now to Him Who is able to do immeasurably more than all we ask or imagine…" (Ephesians 3:20).

Just because we know Him to be the One Who can give us a life of Immeasurably More does not mean that we should not ask or imagine what He can give us and will provide for us. In all my four decades of following and walking with Jesus, I have always had the tendency to look for formulas, patterns, programs, and strategies to implement in my own life to draw closer to Jesus. It was not until recently that I realized that God wants us to write our own recipe or formula for life with Him. What you and Holy Spirit come up with together will be just as unique as your fingerprint and will likely have just as many nuances to it as the number of hairs on your head. With true transformation will come a burning desire to know Him more, to know His power, to guess what His Immeasurably More might look like in your own life, and the desire not only to be seeking Jesus but to clearly See King Jesus for Who He truly is: the Author and Finisher of your faith (Hebrews 12:2).

Formulaic Faith

Please do not make it all this way on the journey to More and not learn to recognize formulaic faith for what it truly is: "religion," not true relationship and intimacy with Holy Spirit. Formulaic Faith is a recipe, plan, curriculum, and strategy that gives the false assurance that upon its completion, you will arrive at intimacy with Christ but does not deliver because it is man-made and Holy Spirit is not invited in to do the supernatural. Formulas, acronyms to follow, 12-step plans, Bible study and reading plans, systematic teaching and the like are all wonderful tools, but they are empty without the supernatural touch of Holy Spirit. They can take you far, can teach you loads of information, and can equip you for ministry. They cannot replace intimacy with Holy Spirit. They produce religious believers who strive to live for Jesus but walk around in Less. Although I participated in these types of formulas year after year for decades, none of them allowed me to see the More that Holy Spirit offers. None equipped me to shatter the walls and ceiling of my spiritual development cube. Dying to self, repentance, and asking Holy Spirit to be Lord is essential. You can come up with your own formula, though, and writing your own recipe with Holy Spirit will give you supernatural wisdom, discernment, understanding of Scripture, understanding of His Kingdom, and exponential growth in your intimacy with Him.

How To Write Your Own Recipe

Have you ever created a recipe before? I have a few times. Cheesy Ricey Chicken was my favorite. It was developed by this girl almost thirty years ago when I was a poor college student. It had three ingredients, and I bet you can guess what they were. The amazing thing about asking Holy Spirit to help you write your very own one-of-a-kind recipe for More is that it will fit and suit you perfectly, it will have the flexibility to be modified as you shift from one season of life to another, and it will not only satisfy you, but it will leave you wanting more at the same time. I still have not figured out how that works, but I know it is true. The more I get to know Holy Spirit, the more irresistible He becomes.

There are many ways to go about writing your own recipe for More, and only you can write your own, but consider what you want the result of your recipe to be for those around you as your walk with the Lord impacts your world. Just like cinnamon and the quantity can greatly impact the flavor of a cookie or pie, so will how much Scripture reading or memorization will impact your recipe for spiritual growth. Do you prefer your oatmeal cookies with or without raisins? Well, some people will want to include online teaching from YouTube and the like, and others will want to limit the teachings of others to books and live messages. Salt is another ingredient that can make or break a recipe. Maybe the time you spend in the Word is your "salt": a little will make a difference, but the more you add, the more flavor you will taste.

What "flavor" do you want the outcome of your spiritual development for the future to have? Do you want it to taste and smell like grace, mercy, humility, compassion? A little of all of these or primarily *compassion*, and less like evangelism? That is for you to seek out Holy Spirit and determine from Him. Religion says we have to be doing things a certain way. Religion usually says we all have to be sharing the Gospel every day with everyone, even if we are in quarantine with only our cat. More with Holy Spirit is evident in the freedom He gives us to figure out how we are fearfully and wonderfully made in His image and grow in grace and the knowledge of Him. He equips us to use our gifts and talents to impact the unique world He has placed us into.

I challenge you to sit down and figure out what you want your relationship with Holy Spirit to look like and seek Him to show you how you will grow into that. There is no legalism here, though. You don't even have to write your recipe down. Asking Holy Spirit for His wisdom in developing it is essential, though.

Let me outline two tools you can use to write your own recipe for spiritual development. The first, straight from Scripture, is found in Acts 3. The second is a smorgasbord of choices with countless combinations of elements for you to choose and customize your personal plan. The plan is not the end-all-be-all of this exercise. The goal is who you will be in five years from now, or maybe seven or ten, which is what we will discuss after you explore the tools that can lead you to More.

Here is a big checklist primarily taken from Acts 3. Do not expect to grow deeper using this unless you have asked Holy Spirit to partner with you in this process.

10 Steps to Intimacy with Holy Spirit:

1. Draw near to God (through prayer and the reading of the Word) (James 4:8).

2. Receive power (ask Holy Spirit to fill you afresh regularly) (Acts 1:8).

3. Be amazed (go looking for signs and wonders in the lives of those around you and/or on social media) (Acts 3:1–10).

4. Be perplexed. (Ask questions, even absurd ones.) (Acts 3:11–18)

5. Repent (Acts 3:19).

6. Return to Him (Acts 3:19).

7. Experience times of refreshing (Acts 3:19).

8. Seek His presence more and more (Acts 3:19).

9. Experience restoration (Acts 3:21).

10. Seek first the kingdom, and all these things shall be added to you (Matthew 6:33).

Choose Your Own Ingredients for Spiritual Development

Throughout forty years of following and walking with Jesus, my spiritual growth has looked different in each season. First, I encourage you to identify the season of life you are currently in (not an exhaustive list):

High school	Step-parenting
College	Adoptive parent
Singleness	Separated
Early marriage	Divorced
Working a job	Widowed
Career	Married, separate lives
Grad student	Dealing with illness
Entrepreneur	Financial struggle
Church ministry	Wealth
Remarried	Dealing with trauma
Mid-marriage	Dealing with abuse
Early parenting	Dealing with an ill child
Parenting young	Celebrity spotlight

Regardless of which season you are in, just talk to the Lord about this and ask Holy Spirit to help you see who He wants to be for you in this season of life. Give yourself grace and patience to work within the schedule and constraints that have been placed on you at your particular age and stage. He does not expect you to ignore your responsibilities, just the distractions the bad father sends your way. Ask Holy Spirit to help you identify your distractions. Identifying where you are in your journey through life will help you write your own recipe that will produce a relationship where you "taste and see that the Lord is good" (Psalm 34:8).

If you could choose 1–3 of the following (try to narrow it down), which characteristic or name for God do you most closely relate to:

Lord	Glorious
Healer	Holy
Wonderful Counselor	Righteous
Peace Giver	Victor
Savior	Deliverer
Friend	Shield and Defense
Helper	King of Kings
Comforter	Emmanuel
Guardian	Yahweh
Shepherd	Adonai
Everything	Papa
Best Friend	Provider
Omnipotent	Curator
Omniscient	Lover
Omnipresent	Teacher
Strong Tower	Creator

Taking the time to identify this should give you insight into the questions you may have for Holy Spirit. The names that you do not choose may lead you to ask questions about His character and plan for your life. He is all of these and *so much more*. Choose one or two to seek after. Look for these in scripture. Ask Holy Spirit in prayer to reveal to you a part of God's nature that you have never considered before.

After you have identified where you are in life, recognize the unique characteristics of your own current lifestyle, and identify attributes or More of God that you would like to discover. Then, write your own recipe by choosing two or more of the following "ingredients" and start practicing them daily or weekly as you can. Seek Holy Spirit through a combination of the following:

Choose One Increment of Time + Two Or More Others

Time	Love Language	By Sight	By Hearing
2 min	Listening	Written word	Preaching
5 min	Giving	God's creation	Teaching
15 min	Serving	Man's creation	Christian music
30 min	Comforting	People	Conversation
60 min	Affirming	Performance	Recitation
Varying amounts			

By Touch	By Taste	By Smell	Habits
Hugs	Communion	Incense	Fasting
Handshakes	Feasting	Prepared food	Being generous
Laying on of hands	Celebrations	New life	Worship
	Whole foods	New growth	Scripture memory
			Seeking Righteousness
			Special skills
Tradition	Shared Interest	Prayer	Sacrifice
Assemble	People	Adoration	Giving when it hurts
Sing	Places	Confession	Letting go of chains
Baptism	Things	Reverence	Praising when it hurts
	Activities	Intercession	Giving time
	Work/labor	Petitions	
		Seeking the Kingdom	

Start today. Start now. Set the book down for a bit and seek His face. Ask Him to be present with you. Call on His name. Start with two minutes; next week, make it five, and next month, maybe it will be thirty. Start tithing this Sunday, start giving extra to your favorite ministry next paycheck, and maybe next year, give till it hurts. Start moving toward

Holy Spirit. Draw near to God, and you will begin to see More when you come to Him with a pure heart, clean hands, and a desire to be in His presence. If you spend ten minutes with Him today and only two minutes with Him tomorrow—*no big deal*. Just start back at two and keep adding minutes. If you break His heart by falling back into Less, repent, return, ask Him for restoration. Scripture says, "The steadfast love of the Lord never ceases; His mercies never come to an end; they are new every morning; great is Your faithfulness!" (Lamentations 3:22–23, ESV), but I have discovered that, in fact, His mercies are new *every moment*, no need to wait until tomorrow morning to repent, return, and be restored.

Please do not be mad or frustrated (but let's face it, you probably will be) when you don't see a difference tomorrow or next week. Transformation looks different for different people. Don't forget your fingerprint. You are unique. You may start hearing the whisper of Holy Spirit in the car, shower, while you are cooking, while you are in line at a drive-thru, or waiting at the DMV (yes, it is possible). You may connect some dots in Scripture this Christmas or Easter and notice how descriptions of God's power start popping off the page when you read. It may not be until next Christmas that you are stunned by the actual reality of Emmanuel: God *is* with us. Discovering More is a process, and the goal is not to see more tomorrow or to receive the tickets to that event you have always wanted to go to for your 40th birthday, but the most important goal is who you will be in five years.

You in Five Years

More comes here, there, a little bit now, a little bit later, a lot on the most random day possible, or with a big build-up of anticipation over weeks, months, and maybe years. Look for More, and you will start seeing it. Look for it in today, but look for it in yesterday, too. Ask God to give you hindsight into how He led you through circumstances, how He provided in difficult times, and how He blessed you and poured out favor when you got the job you always wanted, were accepted to the university you knew was perfect for you, or discovered that you have the absolute best cat in the whole world that you would not have found had He not redirected your path to the animal shelter on that specific day.

The you that you see in the mirror in five years will be the result of the choices you make to "seek first the kingdom of God and His righteousness" today. Delayed gratification may be the hardest part of More. The man or woman that you were in your cube was taught and shaped to seek immediate results. Our enemy has led us to believe that the sprint is more important than the marathon. God is not in a hurry. He is more interested in who you are becoming than how many pounds you can shed in a month or how much money you can make in six. Everyone trying to sell you a strategy or plan will promise results in a year or less, and congratulations to you if you achieve them. God is not interested in the results of a strategy, formula, or plan. God is interested in your heart and in the fruit you will bear. Fruit does not grow overnight; have you noticed? Fruit needs multiple seasons and stages to develop to maturity, ripen, and bless the person who consumes it with intense, delicious flavor. You will be hard-pressed to find a tree that will produce fruit in less than three years, and the average is 4–5. The more mature the tree, the sweeter the fruit. Once you find yourself free from religion, tradition, instant gratification that Less promises, and any other entanglements, pick yourself up and plant yourself by the streams of living water found in Scripture and Holy Spirit (Psalm 1:3). Graft yourself into the true vine of Jesus Christ (John 15:4).

"He will be like a tree firmly planted by streams of water, which yields fruit in its season and its leaf does not wither; and in whatever he does, he prospers" (Psalm 1:3).

This passage says that a "tree is planted," not a seed. We have to be uprooted from the life the world, and our sin nature has directed our growth. We must transplant ourselves or intentionally replant ourselves from our cube where the ground is fertile, and the living water flows. Putting roots down into the fertile soil of God's Word will establish you, ground you, and strengthen you in a way that the "stage" your life was once on never could. Great security comes with growing your life on the foundation of God's word. As this metaphor of your life as a tree is explored, you can see that the stream of living water is Jesus Christ and Holy Spirit is Christ in you, the hope of glory (Colossians 1:27). Being hydrated by Him gives abundant, vibrant life and allows you to be nourished. This placement produces the fruit of the Spirit in your life as described in Galatians 5:22–23: love, joy, peace, longsuffering, gentleness, goodness, faith, meekness, and temperance. In doing so, you feed and nourish others. Fruit also bears seeds that can be scattered throughout the Earth to reproduce fruit in the lives of others.

"I am the vine, you are the branches; he who abides in Me and I in him, he bears much fruit, for apart from Me you can do nothing" (John 15:5).

Quite simply, once you are planted, stay put. Abide. Hide your life within the life of Christ (Colossians 3:3). Practically, that means that once you have figured out your own recipe, cook it up consistently, whether that is hourly, daily, or weekly. If you remain in God's word and actively seek Him, you will bear spiritual fruit. John 15 promises it. However, nothing of eternal value can be done apart from Him.

As we begin to understand the More that God has in store for us and as we begin to follow the recipe we have written with Holy Spirit, a door will open within your spirit, like the wardrobe that the Pevensie children stepped into in C.S.

Lewis's *The Lion, Witch and the Wardrobe*, to the Kingdom of God. The exchange of Less for More comes with a new perspective on life. "…the kingdom of heaven is at hand" (Matthew 3:2). It is time to explore the Kingdom! Join me!

Chapter 20

Imagine you have been married for about eighteen months or so, and it is Christmas time. You and your spouse are living paycheck to paycheck most months, but a little money has been set aside for gifts. No children grace your home yet. The decorations have been hung, all of the church services and special programs have occurred, and the family dinner is complete. The year is 2010, and you are an avid coffee drinker who has been hoping and praying that your spouse would buy you a Keurig coffee maker since they don't drink coffee and you feel it wasteful to make extra coffee every day that ends up down the drain. Buying yourself a Keurig at this time is out of the question—just too frivolous. You are committed to being a good steward of the coffee maker you have and will be thankful for it. You and your spouse decide to exchange gifts on Christmas Eve. You sit near the tree and are aware of the fact that a perfect memory is being created. Your spouse hands you a medium-sized box wrapped in festive red and green. They pause to watch you open the gift. After sliding your fingers underneath two small strips of tape and pulling up the flaps of paper, you see a familiar gray box with black and brown writing and accents; you recognize the design; as you continue to pull back paper, you see the word and image you longed to see—Keurig. Your heart fills with excitement and gratitude; you begin to rip the paper now, and quickly, you have sat the box upright on your lap. You notice that your spouse has taken note of your change in expression and your excitement, but their brow has become furrowed. At the moment, you slide the tab out of the cardboard to release the lid, and you hear your spouse say, "There's something else inside." A brief moment later, your smile fades as you look inside the box that does not contain what the image on the outside portrays. No Keurig coffee maker. A lovely gift. A thoughtful gift. A gift that fourteen years later you will not remember because you remember being deceived and that you went another year making coffee with Mr. Coffee.

Many believers today have received the gift of eternal life, but they have not opened the gift to discover what is inside. They have the promise of eternity, but they do not know anything about it. Eternity begins the day you repent and believe. Most believers have received the gift, but have not realized that the Cross is not all there is to the gift of salvation. There is more. Salvation is a door to the gift of eternity. Beyond the glass ceiling of your cube is the Kingdom of God. The Kingdom of God is that which is yet to come when time will be no more. There is more to the Kingdom. The Kingdom is also now. "Thy kingdom come, thy will be done, on earth as it is in heaven" (Matthew 6:10). Now, today. The Kingdom is here. The Kingdom is within you and me because we have Jesus. He is the Kingdom. He is within us. He wants us to rule and reign here and now as we will in eternity. Both now and then. Ask Holy Spirit to open your eyes to the Kingdom. Ask Him to help you see what is beyond the door of the Gospel of His death, burial, resurrection, and return. Jesus was preaching the Gospel of the Kingdom of God before He died, was buried and resurrected. What was Jesus teaching and preaching about while He walked the Earth? The Gospel of the Kingdom of God was His message. We need to know and understand the rest of the Gospel, the Kingdom.

Kingdom teaching was omitted from my spiritual development cube. Verses about the Kingdom were read or quoted, but no exegesis was given; the concept was never unpacked. The question of what it was and why Jesus always talked about it never seemed to come up, either. I find this incredibly strange now. For a word that is used over 125 times in four gospels of the KJV, what reason could there have possibly ever been for leaving it out of the thousands of preaching services I attended? Of course, I cannot remember them all, but I sure do remember a lot of other topics that were mentioned over and over and over. Do you know, have you ever heard a discussion on Matthew 3:2 and John the Baptist proclaiming, "Repent, for the Kingdom of Heaven is at hand"? There was a great emphasis placed on repentance from time to time, particularly during evangelistic tent meetings or week-long "revivals," but today, neither seems to be part of the vocabulary of much of the church in America. How sad.

Sometimes, we sing about it, but mindlessly so. Once again, I doubt anyone is asking about the lyrics they are singing. One of my favorite Christian bands is named We The Kingdom, and yet it never dawned on me to ask why they refer to themselves as such. Most notable is that 99.9 percent of all Christians I know can recite "The Lord's Prayer" and always quote the part, "Thy Kingdom come, Thy will be done, on Earth as it is in Heaven." (Matthew 6:10) and then again end it by saying, "for Yours is the Kingdom, the glory, the power forever. Amen." (vs 13). Once you see and begin to understand the More found within the Kingdom, you cannot unsee it. You will not be the same. An amazing and wonderful joy and excitement will refresh your faith.

Ironically, I have heard as many discussions on the Kingdom from Christian businessmen as I have from a pulpit in my search for answers to my questions: What does the Kingdom look like? Can it be seen? What is my role in the Kingdom? Is the Kingdom past, present, future, or all three? How can I build the Kingdom?

The bad father wants us stuck in Less. Kingdom mindset brings More. Apparently, he has manipulated culture, particularly in America, to such a degree that we have elevated an impotent "sinner's prayer" and are, as a church, leading people to a fake Jesus. We bring them to the cross, but no transformation is taking place. Now, there are many, many believers who do not realize that there is more to "seek" than just salvation and are stuck at the foot of the cross. Their discipleship, if any is offered them, takes them round and round the cross in a box of religion, similar to the one that shaped them, rather than upward, eyes on the Father and eternity, growing ever closer to Him, ever more intimate with Holy Spirit as we "…look to the blessed Hope and the glorious appearing of our great God and Savior, Jesus Christ" (Titus 2:13, NKJV). I know that before I experienced true transformation, I was not looking for His appearance, and definitely would not describe it as glorious in any honest conversation. Messages in the church are about salvation and Christian living, but I have been in very few services in the past two decades that could be described as transformational. I have heard a lot of "good preaching," "sound doctrine," and a call for sinners to respond to the Gospel message, but they are superficial at best. I learned a lot. I took notes and retained a lot. I am very comfortable with the Scriptures and writing my own recipe for spiritual development as a result of decades of preaching, but the power is often non-existent.

The message of salvation is vitally important. Jesus is the Way, the Truth, and the Life, and no one comes to the Father except through Him (John 14:6). "We have all sinned and come short of the glory of God" (Romans 3:23). "For God so loved the world that He gave His only begotten Son that whoever believes in Him will not perish but have eternal life" (John 3:16). "If we confess with our mouth that Jesus is Lord and believe in our heart that God raised Him from the dead, we will be saved" (Romans 10:9–10). This is life or death. This is the only way to Jesus. This is the way of the cross of Christ. But wait, there's More!

Admitting our sins, believing in Jesus, and confessing Jesus as Lord is the door to eternal life. The Kingdom is on the other side of the door. We were never meant to be stuck in the door. God's desire is that we discover His Kingdom through His Spirit's revelation in our lives. "Seek first the Kingdom and His righteousness" (Matthew 6:33). I memorized this verse in elementary school. No one ever explained to me what the Kingdom was and how to seek it until I was forty-four. People must know there's more. There's more, I tell you, there's more. Ask Holy Spirit to confirm in your own spirit that which is Truth about the Kingdom of God.

Examine Exchange Embrace

Seeking Jesus, His Kingdom, and His righteousness are the first steps into More. These three steps will allow you to not only enter His house with fresh eyes, ears, and life but will allow you to finally pull back the veil that was torn at His death on the cross and step into His presence in the Holy of Holies within the tabernacle of your soul. Walking in His ways and following His plan for your life, free of the entanglements that leave you in regret, will guide you to the gift of Immeasurably More that He longs for you to unwrap and discover in moments with Him, in the beauty of a sunset over the ocean, the joy in sledding down fresh powder in the hills of West Virginia, or tasting that perfect cheesecake that you are convinced will be on the table at the wedding feast of the Lamb. So, examine your life to recognize where you were in your walk with the Lord as the cube guided your growth to now, observe the now you are standing in at a crossroads, and choose to continue to walk in Less or exchange it for More.

Examination does not have to, but may require a deconstruction of your faith. Examine the culture you were raised in and live in now. What parts do not line up with Scripture? Does pride cause you to disqualify some people from receiving the Hope you carry with you? Is the soundtrack of your life drawing you away from the Presence of God or toward

Him? Does the church you attend operate more like religion than the Kingdom? Religion limits the power of Holy Spirit to what can be seen and understood. Religion focuses on what we have to do for Christ rather than what He empowers us to do through Him. What about the other characteristics of religion mentioned in Chapter Thirteen? Are those evident in your church? Consider your family and your own habits, traditions, and preferences. What needs to go? Is gossip entangling you? Are you debating things on social media that Holy Spirit can sort out without your help? If you have not already, ask Holy Spirit to show you in what areas you were taught wrong by well-meaning pastors, teachers, and parents who were led into religion themselves by those who shaped their cubes. Once you examine and recognize truth of the Kingdom, truth about Immeasurably More, and the truth of the greatness of God, choose to exchange the Less you are walking in for the More that Holy Spirit wants to manifest in your life.

Since discovering the More that God has planned for my life, I have recognized that the cross of Christ is the very place that we need to make an exchange of Less for More. The exchange of Less for More that Jesus wants for you is a process, and you will continuously discover and trade up for eternity. There is always more that He has in store. In the past few years, I have discovered seven specific treasures that He has allowed me to trade up for in my walk with Him. I pray these will be trade-ups for you as well:

1. Exchange the fear of man for the fear of God.
2. Exchange broken teachers for Holy Spirit as your teacher.
3. Exchange self for His Spirit.
4. Exchange discontent for peace.
5. Exchange striving for thriving.

6. Exchange pride for humility.

7. Exchange poverty for wealth.

Several recommendations for teaching and tools for each of these specific areas of growth can be found in the Appendix. There is much to be learned, and many can speak with strong authority on these subjects. Each will help break off the chains that hold you to the old man lifestyle and will equip you to walk as the new creation that you were transformed into. Please know, though, that you will live and operate at the level of your teachers. Holy Spirit should always be your ultimate teacher, but you should also seek out wisdom from those who are walking closely with Holy Spirit and ask Him to give you discernment as to who to be taught by.

Anyone who has worked with young children for any length of time will often recognize that there are different ways to approach children. When you meet them for the first time, different factors will impact whether or not you bond with them, develop mutual respect, relate to them, and have the potential to influence them. Although there are many uncontrollable factors, a huge one that you can control is embracing and accepting them. Embracing children is the overt means of representing the emotional connection of accepting them. An embrace, most often as a hug, conveys so much to a child and in the right timing can establish the foundation for the opportunity to influence them, mold and make them into who God wants them to be. Parents have the opportunity to embrace and accept their children on a daily basis, but the foundation is laid in the first embrace in the child's infancy.

Jesus longs to embrace you with More. Will you return His embrace and accept the More He is offering you? Will you embrace all of Him? Are you willing to accept the parts of Scripture that were omitted in your faith tradition? Are you willing to explore what you do not understand? Are you willing to embrace the teaching of the Kingdom that has been ignored by many in the church? He wants you to embrace:

1. *All* of Him
2. His Ways and plans (Isaiah 55:8–9)
3. His will
4. His Word in full
5. His thoughts.

Once you embrace Him, submit to Him, recognize His Holiness, and decide that His Truth will trump your own, then "all these things will be added to you." Let's finish this journey of discovery by unpacking the gift of More He is handing us. Let's figure out the More that He has in store for you. Let's walk through the door into More.

Chapter 21

But wait, there's More. More to me will not be more to you, but more is more. Holy Spirit wants to show you the more that He has uniquely designed for you. Start looking for it, and you will find it. Sometimes, you will have to stop and W.A.I.T. before you can see the More. Are you willing to wait on More? Stop, look, and listen like you would at the railroad crossing. There are four things you can do to prepare your heart to see, hear, and embrace the more that God has for you once you have been transformed through belief and repentance.

Wonder.

Be in **A**we.

Investigate.

Test Holy Spirit.

"When I consider the Your heavens, the work of Your fingers, the moon and the stars, which You have ordained; what is man that You take thought of Him, and the son of man that You care for him?" (Psalm 8:3). This is what it means to have faith like a child. Take the time to explore and discover Holy Spirit, the power in Jesus Christ, and the ultimate goodness of Father God. Take time to wonder, like the first time you went to the zoo or a circus and saw the magnificent animals He created. Ask who, what, where, why, when, and how of everything. Be in awe like the first time you were mesmerized by a waterfall. Investigate like the first time you played in the snow and realized that you could use it to move on, build with, and dance in. Test Him like the first time you prayed and believed He would provide the means for you to see your family for Christmas that year you lived on the other side of the country for school. Get to know Him beyond what is told to you, explained for you, and the answered prayers you have witnessed in the lives of others. Ask Him to reveal Himself to You and then W.A.I.T. on Him to do so.

Once you are comfortable in the WAIT, there are two ways I have found to recognize More. The process certainly does not have to be scripted, though. Just like your fingerprint, Holy Spirit will speak to you in a way that is uniquely for you. He wants you to write your own recipe for intimacy, but He wants intimacy. He wants you to know Him deeply and know that You can always go deeper. There is no end to the More you can discover in Him. If you need some help recognizing More, you can choose one of these acronyms to help your spiritual eyes open to what He is doing in, through, and around you.

M.O.R.E. #1

Mindset on Righteousness and Eternity

Reframe your brain. Rewire your thinking to that which is Righteous and that which is eternal. Colossians 3:2 says, "Set your mind on things above." Choose to focus on that which is around you, representing the message of Phillippians 4:8–9: "…that which is pure, lovely, of good report." You will likely have to ask Holy Spirit to help with this. This will not come naturally. He will help you to recognize lies and choose truth. He will allow you to see when you are stepping into chaos and help you choose order. He will illuminate the path that leads to success over that which will entangle you in Less. As you ask Him to help you choose well and choose that which pleases and honors Him, you will also find it easier to choose that which impacts for eternity rather than that which is perishing. A mind set on the eternal will invest in that which impacts lives for eternity, will pursue endeavors that establish the Kingdom of God on Earth, and will worship the Lord in His presence as we will in heaven. Worship without inviting the presence of

God is pointless. Worship requires a mind set on His Holiness, not a mind set on performance, production, or experience.

M.O.R.E. #2

"M" Is for Mind of Christ

Although His ways are higher, we can know His heart and His mind through intimacy with Holy Spirit. More understanding, knowledge, wisdom, and discernment will come to you as you seek to know Him. To know Him is to want to know Him more, and He will give you the ability to navigate life well as you gain the mind of Christ.

"O" Is for Overflow of Blessing

Delight yourself in the Lord, and He will give you the desires of your heart. He will give you the job/work/business that you have always been drawn to, and you won't care how much you get paid for it, but He will provide for your every need through it. He may give you the home or car that has always been a dream for you. Our family has the literal best cat in the whole world, and she was truly an answer to a specific prayer. He will give you a spouse who becomes your best friend. He may allow you to experience that concert or championship game that you always dreamed about going to. He may give you the ability to "order anything off of the menu" rather than that which is under $20. He will definitely bless you with peace, contentment, hope, grace, and mercy to an extent that you never thought possible.

"R" Is for Revelation and the Riches of His Grace

God will allow you to see beyond the natural. The revelation He will give you may be described as wisdom and knowledge that I described as having the mind of Christ, but He often allows you to "see" supernaturally by recognizing an outcome is coming before it actually does. This may come in the form of recognizing the path that your child is taking will allow them to have success in school. This may come in the form of having peace that a certain illness will not lead to death in a loved one. This may come by knowing that revival is coming to a certain individual or group of Believers. You may reduce this idea to Faith and the truth in Hebrews 11:1: "Now faith is the assurance of things hoped for and the evidence of things unseen." The biggest difference, maybe the only difference in revelation, is recognizing that Holy Spirit is the reason you have the assurance, not anything that you mustered up within yourself.

"E" Is For Everything You Never Knew You Always Wanted.

I am just discovering the everything I never knew I always wanted, so I cannot possibly know yours, but I can tell you that it is the wish list that God creates for you. Just like the Christmas list I wrote out as a nine-year-old with night-and-day Barbie, I am discovering a "list" of things that He always knew He wanted to give me, and I just had to walk in His plan for my life to receive them. I recently began a list of these and easily began the list with about fifteen. A few of them are my third daughter (had my heart set on boys for years), the opportunity to live in Indonesia from 2006–2008, owning a farm and turning it into a community of ministry, becoming an "adopted" daughter of Marshall University, a wedding in the desert, and a unique God-designed experience I had at Mt. St. Helens.

I wish I had come up with the phrase: "Everything I never knew I always wanted." I did not, but ever since hearing Matthew Perry's character, Alex Whitman, speak it in the movie *Fools Rush In* in a movie theater in small-town North Carolina in 1997, it haunted me until my spiritual eyes were opened in 2018. Since then, I see it everywhere. Blessing upon blessing. More and More.

There is more to know. Go figure out what it is. There is

more to learn. Start studying. There is more to receive. Open your hands. Spread your arms wide to receive the embrace of our Creator. There is more to give and share. Find someone who can be blessed by the more God has given you. There is more to see. Open your physical eyes and ask Holy Spirit to open your spiritual eyes. There is more to understand. Listen, realize, and recognize what God is doing all around you. There is more to do: more ways to serve, more ways to minister, more ways to build the Kingdom, more ways to grow, more fruit to bear, more ways to go into all the world and preach the good news of the Kingdom. There is more to pray for; intercede for others. There are more giftings in the Spirit that you may not be aware of. There are more gifts of experience. There is more peace you can feel. There are more material gifts He will bless you with. There is more amazing food and drink to taste. There are more ways to succeed than what you have known till now.

But wait, there's More.

Epilogue

Have you been invited into God's house? If you haven't, consider yourself invited. Come and see, experience what you may have never recognized was inside before. God's house is probably not what you expect. When you arrive, you will see that it is a place to live, not so much a cathedral, chapel, or church building. Maybe you believed that He prefers such things. He invites you into the home where He resides—a dwelling, a residence, a place where His life unfolds before His beloved children.

Walking up to the door, you may not be impressed with what you see on the outside. The yard will be beautifully manicured but simple or maybe described as ordinary. Your focus may move to the window as you catch a glimpse of the interior. Intriguing. It will probably seem smaller than the mansion you were expecting. The neighborhood may capture your attention next. God's house is here? Clean and classically designed with all of the standard features, the outside humbly represents what is held within. If any feature will captivate your attention as you walk closer, it will be the door.

The door of God's house is the most notable feature by far. The unique construction of the door may not be noticeable from a street view, but as you walk closer, it may take your breath away. The door is impressive in its construction and design. This door is strong. This door is made from reclaimed wood. This door is heavy. You may even notice the hinges—the strongest, most indestructible material you can imagine. This door has a design unlike any you have seen before because it is undeniably a cross. A perfect man gave His life to construct this door.

Many, I dare say most, get stuck here, right on the stoop of the door of God's house. They may get stuck examining the construction and design of the door and house. Some check their map or address notes to make sure they truly found the Father's house. Some start a conversation with others at the door and rehash how they came to find the house. This house surprises many, and they second-guess whether or not they are in the right place. Others may be distracted by activity happening in the front yard or in the street. God's house is at the crossroads of a major thoroughfare: at the corner of More Avenue and Less Way. You may even see public performances, concerts, riots, or theatrical demonstrations going on just beyond the sidewalk, perhaps in the middle of the street. Many get distracted looking back, sometimes at the very last second, before they reach for the door handle.

Although much effort and sacrifice went into the design and construction of the house and its front door, the door is never locked, and opening the door to step inside has been made incredibly simple: step through the cross. The door looks so heavy and cumbersome but is so light and easy in reality. The noise and distractions usually intensify, growing louder at this point. Those who do not know how to get inside will distract others from doing so with every fiber of their beings. You've been in the world for so long that it is hard to ignore the familiar and exchange it for the unfamiliar, no matter how inviting. Familiarity can easily rob you of the highest and best that was intended for you. God's house will amaze you. God's house is everything you never knew you always wanted. Setting your eyes on the cross will guide you through the threshold. Surrendering the familiar and natural for the supernatural of this home, taking a step of faith, and realizing you can never afford, design, or build a house such as this on your own—without the Master Builder Jesus Christ. Open the door and step inside the House of the Lord.

Once inside, you are family, you belong, and you are safe and secure. Regardless of whether or not you ever step outside of the house, you will always belong. You are forever changed. You can leave and return as often as you choose, but you will never be just a guest again. Each time you step through the door will be easier, as long as you do not try to bring the world with you. The Father encourages you to go out and invite others to come back with you. Leaving is not a problem at all. Come and go often. He will go with you, of course. The Spirit remains inside you when you are outside of His house. Just don't stay in the world for too long during any one excursion. Be sure to come home. Hearing the Spirit speak becomes harder and harder out in the world with so many distractions. The noise of our enemy gets so, so loud. Remember that we are to be in the world, but we are not supposed to operate like the world. Our source of strength and protection comes from within. We need not create our own protection or vehicle. Just walk throughout the world listening to His voice within you and carry your Sword. We need to go out and seek the broken, lost, and hurting and bring them home, to the Father's house. We need to see them and be sure they know that He sees them, too.

Inside, I pray you feel a flood of peace. Welcome Home! Inside, you will likely first see the foyer; you may just call it an entryway or the hall. You will likely be surprised by how many people are there but how there is still room for many more. This room never gets full or even crowded. There is always room for more. Looking around, you will notice the eclectic decor. The variety will somehow not be surprising. God lets His children bring in their favorite pictures, music, trinkets, and furniture. They are tastefully arranged but represent quite a mashup of cultures, customs, and preferences. You will notice doorways into other rooms and will possibly recognize the entryway to the living room, den, and kitchen. The large hand-crafted staircase at the end of the hall may catch your attention and raise more questions in your mind about where you have found yourself and, of course, where that staircase leads. If you are like me, you expected one large room with uncomfortable chairs, benches, and a platform of some kind on the far end. You will not find those in God's house. God's house is warm and inviting and a place where relationships grow and thrive. When you were invited to God's house, perhaps you were given that description rather than what is actually found here.

I hope you will step into God's living room. Don't get stuck in the foyer. Imagine the most comfortable and welcoming room you have ever experienced, and consider what it would be like to be amazed and in awe of the love and peace you feel there. Imagine a room where family gathers to share stories of Him and sing songs to Him. You may be surrounded by people you have never met before, but they will likely be people with whom you have an instant, deep soul connection. Picture a room large and welcoming but not so crowded that you feel your personal space invaded. All of the best seating is available: couches, chairs, floor, chaise. Sit wherever you are most comfortable. Close to Him or with others between you and Him. It matters not because His presence reaches every corner, every inch, floor to ceiling.

Sitting in this room, you may notice emblems of royalty. In this room, you recognize princes and princesses gathered around, face to face, sharing precious moments of faith. Lean back in a chair and feel at home, rest in the presence of the family of our Father. Worship Him with your words, thoughts, and song. Celebrate. Reflect. There will be a sweet, sweet Spirit among us. Do you hear joy? If it is possible to hear joy, I hear joy there. If it is possible to hear peace, I hear peace. If it is possible to hear life, I hear life. If it is possible to hear God's glory, I hear His glory in the testimony and praises of His people. Do you see what I see? If it is possible to see Hope, I see

Hope. If it is possible to see Grace, I see Grace. If it is possible to see Mercy, I see Mercy. If it is possible to see satisfaction, I see satisfaction. Do you feel what I feel? If it is possible to touch honor, I am touching the honor of God. If it is possible to touch unity, I am touching unity as I sit and soak in His presence. If it is possible to touch freedom, I am touching freedom, and I can feel it radiate through my body. If it is possible to touch the immortal and invisible, then I am doing exactly that in God's living room.

Finding anyone who stays in the Father's living room all of the time is rare. No one would comment on such, but in the nature of our humanity, attention span, and other physical needs of Earth, our brothers and sisters will come and go from this sacred space at their own discretion. I would encourage you to step back into the foyer after a while and see who has arrived or who has camped out there in the hallway. More and more family are likely to arrive regularly. Certain time frames are busier than others—Sundays are the busiest, of course, and draw the biggest crowds. The foyer is where they gather on Sundays, mostly. Brothers and sisters will likely be there reminiscing and catching up with one another. Once you recognize and identify the sweet Spirit you will feel it everywhere. I usually stand back against the wall and spend a few moments relishing in the refreshing feeling of the homecoming. Make no mistake: all come together freely. There is no air of obligation or duty, but sincere service and sacrifice will be prevalent.

Be sure to explore the rest of the house. My favorite is the Family Room, or Den as some call it. Somehow, it is more intimate than even the living room. The lights are usually a bit dimmer. The Son is there, and the siblings seem to stay a little closer to each other. Unlike the formal living room, I tend to communicate best with my Father there, through the Son. I hear His voice more clearly, more specifically, more intimately. He speaks right to me, and I am sure He will speak to you as well. Tears flow more freely in the family room, but no one seems to mind. The reason for tears ranges across the whole spectrum of emotions, convictions, and feelings. I cried out of joy, relief, and the overwhelming satisfaction of His embrace the first time I visited there. He and I have had moments kind of like this one before in the living room, but only in small short, almost hurried encounters. The experience is sweeter in the Family Room because time melts away and I am able to catch my breath, savor, and soak it all in.

The other most common areas of the house to spend time in would be the kitchen, rest room, and bedroom. These rooms are the most unlike the traditional homes that we live in, but I would encourage you to visit them. Visit them in any order and at any time. You will love spending time in the kitchen, whether you are preparing a feast for others or partaking of the feast yourself. Worshiping the Father here is simply serving others in the House. This happens outside of His house, as well as in the kitchen, but here, there are fewer distractions, interruptions, and mishaps—none, as a matter of fact. Service in His house seems to be protected from all of the stumbling blocks we seem to experience in the world. The bedrooms are always available when you need rest, or just some quiet. Our Father will come in to you and meet you there. These rooms allow isolation from the world and others. They are safe, secure, and completely restorative. Restrooms are where you can wash the world off of you and clean up. Some people call them repentance rooms.

Return to the foyer anytime. His presence can be felt there almost any time. Brothers and sisters have sweet fellowship there. Some enjoy this so much that they never go into the living room, family room, kitchen, restrooms, or bedrooms. No one goes upstairs unless the Father calls them there. There's more to explore, though. I have not experienced all of the many rooms He has prepared for us. Go explore. He wants you to discover more.

The original never-*end*ing story.

Appendix

Recommended Further Reading

1. *The Awe of God* by John Bevere
2. *I Declare War* by Levi Lusko
3. *The Blue Parakeet* by Dr. Scot McKnight
4. *Out of the Rut, Into Revival* by A.W. Tozer
5. *The Pursuit of God* by A.W. Tozer
6. *Dangerous Jesus*, Kevin Burgess
7. *Last Supper on the Moon* by Levi Lusko
8. *Kingdom Principles: Preparing for Kingdom Experience and Expansion* by Myles Munroe

Endnotes

Introduction

1. Charles Dickens, "Charles Dickens Quote," Quotefancy, accessed April 4, 2024, https://quotefancy.com/quote/11877/Charles-Dickens-It-was-the-best-of-times-it-was-the-worst-of-times-it-was-the-age-of.

Chapter 1

Chapter 2

Chapter 3

1. George Keith, "How Firm a Foundation ye Saints of the Lord," 1787.

2. John Crist, "Lady Who Has a Bible Verse for Every Situation," uploaded by John Crist April 30, 2017, https://youtu.be/hzEL4h1vq7o?si=UgLIeYKbtebUX74H, accessed April 4, 2024.

Chapter 4

Chapter 5

Chapter 6

1. "Roadblock—Don't give strangers your address: A G.I.Joe PSA," uploaded by @PSAGIJoe on March 9, 2010, https://youtu.be/vFthiZ_Jftc?si=933XV-Om5ISdKS1u, accessed April 11, 2023.

2. Helen Lemmel, "Turn Your Eyes Upon Jesus," 1922.

Chapter 7

Chapter 8

Chapter 9

1. *Ferris Bueller's Day Off*, directed by John Hughes (Paramount Pictures, 1986).

Chapter 10

Chapter 11

1. Victor Hugo, "To love another person is to see the face of God," Goodreads, accessed February 20, 2024, https://www.goodreads.com/quotes/49720-to-love-another-person-is-to-see-the-face-of.

2. Robert Cull, "Open My Eyes, Lord," Maranatha Music, 1976.

Chapter 12

1. Thomas Studd, "Only one life, twill soon be past. Only what's done for Christ shall last," Reasons for Hope Jesus, accessed April 9, 2024, https://reasonsforhopejesus.com/only-one-life-twill-soon-be-past-by-c-t-studd-1860-1931/.

Chapter 13

Chapter 14

1. Christine Caine, "Grab a Shovel and Start Digging," Passion 2020, Atlanta, Georgia, January 6, 2020, https://youtu.be/0Ai2ukyggLo?si=Oj44ym_zfI2_CnxF, accessed February 13, 2024.

Chapter 15

1. *Batman Vs. Superman: Dawn of Justice*, directed by Zack Snyder (Warner Brothers Pictures, 2016).

Chapter 16

Chapter 17

Chapter 18

1. Dottie Peoples, "He's An On-Time God," On Time God (Atlanta International, 1996).

Chapter 19

Chapter 20

Chapter 21

1. *Fools Rush In*, directed by Andy Tennant (Columbia Pictures, 1997).

Epilogue

About the Author

Donna Nash is a zealous follower of Jesus Christ who is thrilled to see her life-long dream of becoming a published author come to fruition. She longs to see revival in the Church and Jesus Christ lifted high. Her ministry is focused at home on her husband and daughters. With her heart to serve, she volunteers at her daughters' school, leads Bible study, assists her husband with real estate deals, and is learning what it means to be a "theater mom." She loves to travel, drink coffee with friends, and learn new things.